planted

Bottlebrush

planted

Andy Sturgeon

Color photography by
Lorry Eason

Black & white portraits by
Michael Wildsmith

SOMA
san francisco

The author would like to thank Natalie Meddings and especially Charlotte Barton for her never-ending phone calls, hard work and for letting it ruin her life.

Text © 1998 Andy Sturgeon
Photographs © 1998 Lorry Eason/Millennium
and Michael Wildsmith/Millennium

First published in Great Britain 1998 by Hodder & Stoughton. North American edition published 1998 by Soma Books, by arrangement with Hodder & Stoughton.

Soma Books is an imprint of Bay Books & Tapes, Inc., 555 De Haro, No. 220, San Francisco, CA 94107.

Printed in Hong Kong
10 9 8 7 6 5 4 3 2 1

ISBN 1-57959-029-2

Designed by Morag Myerscough at Studio Myerscough

Library of Congress Cataloging-in-Publication Data

Sturgeon, Andy
    Planted/Andy Sturgeon:color photography by Lorry Eason;
  black & white portraits by Michael Wildsmith.--North American ed.
      p.   cm.
    Includes index.
    ISBN 1-57959-029-2 (pbk. : alk. paper)
    1. Gardening.   I. Title.
  SB453.S77 1998   98-33714
  635--dc21   CIP

The publishers would like to thank
Garson Farm Garden Centre, Jim Dick, Marion Sturgeon, Neil Sturgeon, Raymond (wallabies), W. Godfrey and Sons Ltd, The Wildlife Rescue Centre – Cobham, Royal Horticultural Society Garden Wisley, Olive Eason, Duncan Bullen, Francesca Edwards, Yuki Miyake, Debbie Moller, Charlene Mullen, Ia Hjärre, Mary and Grant Epps, Ishbel Myerscough, Kate Reich, Oscar and Louis Davidson, Niall O'Leary, Anne Fullam, John Wildsmith, Graham and Ruth Fraser, Carys Ridsdale, Nick Galvin, Ben and Craig, Paddy Towell and Martin Lee, Lynn Bresler, Anne Askwith, Diana Riley, Alasdair Oliver, Jonathan Fensom, Mrs Carroll, Joanna Tomlinson, The Garden Picture Library (Chinese wisteria, page 99 and burning bush, page 94), Ian and Izita Kerr and Kate Burrett

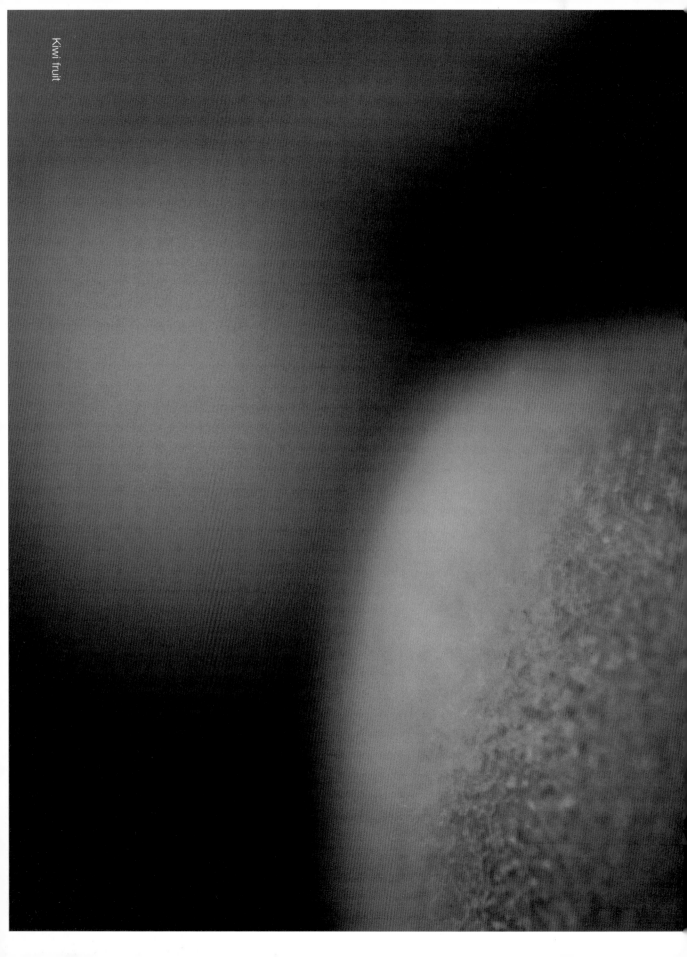
Kiwi fruit

contents

introduction

I first got into gardening at school when I was about eight. I shared a small patch with a friend and I loved planting things, growing vegetables and getting my knees dirty. In truth we weren't actually very good at it. Most of the flowers we lovingly nurtured turned out to be weeds and we were quite lucky not to poison our entire families with green potatoes, but that didn't seem to matter. Ten years later I couldn't think of anything else to say during the careers interview; while my friend, on the other hand, doesn't have a garden to this day.

And now I love it. I think there's something very primal about growing things; being in touch with nature without needing to grow facial hair. The point is – gardening is good news. It's deeply therapeutic and relaxing. It's creative and personal and immensely satisfying.

Perhaps you already have horticultural leanings. Maybe a limp pot of basil on the kitchen windowsill and a straggly spider plant in the bathroom. Often people claim to know nothing about gardening and seem scared to start. But that's the whole point. You don't have to know anything. The thing is not to take it too seriously; do the parts you like and leave the parts you don't. Give it a shot and don't be afraid of making a complete fool of yourself.

This book will guide you through the basics of getting started in your garden. Use it as a reference book to dip into at will. I've put things in a sensible order, from looking to planning to buying to

maintaining, and everything you need to know is here, but get used to flicking back and forth. There's a glossary on page 56 which you may find useful.

There are lots of common terms and techniques that I've left out or adulterated because they're too complicated and time-consuming or just very dull. Hard-core gardeners may be horrified but that's just the way it is. Double digging is out and so are budding and grafting. They may be worthwhile but they're also hard work and as much fun as a bad case of hemorrhoids.

And nearly all the plants I've included here are easy to buy and easy to grow. There are one or two that need a little extra kindness or an urban home away from extreme cold, but they're here because they're worth it to make your garden outstanding. I want this book to be about more than dull, standard bedding plants, and I've assumed that, whether urban or not, your garden isn't vast.

I've practiced organic gardening for several years because it makes sense and my particular form of it is really easy and doesn't involve any hard work. I adopt the basic techniques and then, because I have a small garden, I cut corners and skirt around all the fussy parts. So, I've also written with low maintenance in mind. Gardening should be a pleasure and never a chore – so what we want is a straightforward, effective approach that doesn't ruin your back.

But at the same time, it's as much about the process as the result. Puttering and looking and tweaking and making mental notes for next year and getting your knees dirty – these are the real pleasures.

what you've got

You may have just moved in or perhaps you're fed up with what you've got. Either way, it's time to think positive and liven things up a bit. Have a look at what you have, get to know your garden, its limitations and its advantages – and then think about what it is you want.

Garden style

Your habits and your lifestyle will influence the style of your garden. Are you a minimal modernist or do you like clutter? Are you contemporary or are you chintz? All this is reflected in what you decide to do outside, so identifying your "indoor" style gets you off on the right foot.

Most people want a low-maintenance garden even if they enjoy gardening. It's a fact. But there's more to it than that. You need to think about when you're likely to use the garden, how you're going to use it, and when you're going to do a little bit of work in it.

So what's your job like? Do you get home from work late and use the garden mainly on weekends? Maybe plants that are evening scented would be a good idea. Perhaps you go on vacation every July, in which case don't plant sweet peas and tomatoes that peak then.

You'll probably use the garden for a number of things – but what exactly? Having friends over, in which case you'll need somewhere to sit and somewhere for a barbecue. You might want some cut flowers for the house, and maybe you're a good cook; if so, you should think about space for vegetables and some herbs. Maybe you or your kids need to skateboard over your patio and kick footballs through your ornamentals, so plant something sturdy. Don't forget it's all about quality of life; a little bit of puttering around is therapeutic – but so is lying in a hammock, so plant a couple of trees.

As we'll see in *Structure and Color,* how long you intend to stay in your house will affect what you plant. You also need to think about future plans and additions so you can avoid having to dig things up.

Organics

Now is the time to decide whether you're an organic gardener or not – but have no fear, you don't have to become terribly earnest or go New Age. Organic gardening is a commonsense method of working with, rather than against, nature, of recycling organic waste and encouraging natural pest and disease control instead of spraying chemicals around the place. The end result is a self-contained ecosystem, a haven for wildlife and a source of delicious chemical-free fruit and vegetables. Throughout the book you'll find organic hints and methods. What you won't find is anything about synthetic chemicals. They're expensive, upset the natural balance of the garden and, despite excellent short-term results, they cause tragic long-term effects: plants become more prone to pests and disease and ever-stronger chemicals are needed.

What you've got

First of all take in the atmosphere of your garden. This isn't as easy as it may seem, especially if it's midwinter and you're used to it being something that you occasionally glimpse through the window at weekends. On the other hand, maybe you're too close to it, you're used to seeing it day in, day out, and can't really imagine any change. Whatever the situation, try to think radically – don't put up with stuff just because it's there. Get used to the idea of scrapping a scrubby old apple tree that produced one apple sometime around 1987 and replace it with a magnificent liquid gum. But more about that later.

Oh, and don't chop down the wrong tree – and find that everyone in the next street can now see you getting out of the shower.

Noise

The chances are that you don't have a totally peaceful garden. General noises are hard to control but more specific irritations can be limited. For example an adjacent railroad siding or main road makes one hell of a racket but can be at least partially remedied. A good option is to filter the sound with planting.

Imagine sound as waves. To reduce the amount of noise, these waves must be broken up or absorbed rather than reflected or amplified. To filter or absorb the sound effectively, a barrier of planting a minimum of 16 feet deep is needed. Now this could mean planting your entire garden with shrubs, which is not terribly practical, so what you have to do is a combination of things.

Nonsolid fences and mixed shrub plantings are the best defense and plants with lots of small leaves are better than those with a few large ones. Make the planting as deep as possible, if you have the space, or noise reduction will be negligible. Climbers on trellises above the height of fences can also make a small difference.

In towns, reflected sound is a big problem and one that is most commonly caused by buildings. So you must work out which direction the sound is coming from because it may not be direct from the source. Planting climbers on walls and buildings can reduce reflected sound. Boston ivy is a good one for this because it's self-clinging, it goes high and its many leaves effectively dampen the sound.

Remember, though, noise can only be limited by planting – not eliminated.

Neighbors

Always a problem for some reason: perhaps it's because we're not all meant to live on top of one another. Neighbors come and go; people move far more often in cities than they do in suburban and rural areas. Mark and Nancy are terrific fun at the moment but what happens when they depart for their place in the country and the "neighbor from hell" moves in? I'm afraid you've got to think "worst-case scenario" and plan ahead.

Osteospermum

Cape figwort

Plants take time to grow so if you want to increase your privacy or keep out unwelcome footballs and children, plan it now. A few good thorny shrubs like barberry and holly can be quite effective.

Aspect

Aspect – the direction in which your garden, or more specifically parts of your garden, face. It's probably on the real estate broker's blurb from when you bought the place, although it's amazing how many "south-facing gardens" they think there are. Why? Because a south-facing garden is probably the ideal since it means you can grow the widest range of plants, on the basis that shade can be created but sun can't. So, which way do you face? You could just whip out a compass to find out which way south is but it's just as easy to go outside and have a look. The sun rises in the east and sets in the west, which means at midday it's due south. You need to know all of this when you're deciding what to plant where – what needs sun and what doesn't. Aspect will also influence which areas are dry and which are boggy, so get to know it well.

Have a look to see if trees cast shade over areas and most importantly for how much of the day something is in partial shade or full sun. Remember that the sun is much higher in the sky in summer than it is in winter, which means that things will generally have summer sun for a much longer period each day because it can peer over fences and buildings. Perhaps you need to remove a tree or just its lower branches to let in more light. A deciduous plant (leaves fall off in winter) doesn't care how much shade it's in if it hasn't got any leaves on it; it only cares when it's leafed up in the spring and summer. This is the basis on which many woodland plants survive, doing their stuff in the spring before the overhanging trees get their act together.

Exposure and shelter

Generally, wherever you live there is a prevailing wind. In most cases this won't bother you unless you're particularly exposed and the wind is a cold one blowing from the north or east. In highly built-up areas there is also a funneling effect caused by the geometry of streets and tall buildings, the solid shapes doing nothing to absorb the bitter winter winds that can scorch the leaves of hardy evergreens. Shelter can be created by more resilient plants or by open fences and trellises that filter the wind. Large cities have an artificially raised temperature and the harmful effects of cold winds are partially reduced. However, when siting slightly tender plants bear the wind in mind; several exotic species such as palms and Cape figwort are damaged not only by the cold but by the wind and damp as well.

Climate and microclimate

If you live in a city, particularly a big one, then you will benefit from a phenomenon known as the Urban Heat Blanket. Basically all the asphalt and concrete absorbs the warmth of the sun. Couple that with all the energy emitted by vehicles, homes and industry and you're looking at a 3 to 5 degree bonus wafting around. Those few degrees can have an enormous influence on your plant selection process. You may be able to grow tender things that your country cousins can't. You'll be able to get figs to ripen properly, they won't. Some of your annuals will last through a mild winter, theirs won't; and your trees will have leaves for much longer.

By careful planning and strategic planting we can manipulate the local climate to our benefit and create our own microclimate. We've looked at exposure; creating shelter can reduce wind and its harmful drying effect. Also once your garden is established the plants within it will have a symbiotic relationship. One will shade another from the sun, which may in turn filter the wind or trap moisture around leaves.

Soil, earth, mud

Call it what you like but don't call it "dirt." It's the source of life as we know it in the garden and millions of living organisms call it home. There are five basic types and before you decide what to plant and what to do with your soil you have to figure out which one you've got. If it's not immediately obvious it might mean you've got a middle-of-the-road soil, and with only a bit of effort you can grow whatever you like.

What you want is a nice dark crumbly soil, not too wet, not too dry, with lots of earthworms. It's sort of a mixture of everything.

Clay. Easy to identify this one. It's heavy and difficult to work – the clods are really hard to break up –

drainage is bad and it may easily get waterlogged and smell like rotten eggs. When wet it's slippery and slimy and sticks to your shoes, making you a good six inches taller. When dry it cracks and breaks roots, and if you fall over on it, it hurts like hell. On the plus side it can be turned into a wonderful soil and is normally full of nutrients. Pick up a handful of wet soil and roll it around between your fingers – if you can make it into a cigar shape then you've got clay.

Sand. The opposite of clay really. It has much bigger particles and is a bit like . . . well, sand. It has very good drainage – water disappears almost immediately from the surface – and it's very crumbly. No cigars here I'm afraid. Sandy soils warm up quickly in the spring, which means you can start gardening much earlier and flowers and some fruits tend to mature sooner. On the downside, it will suffer from drought in warm weather and in wet weather all the nutrients get washed out of it, and it can form a hard "cap," which the more wimpy seedlings can't push through when they're embarking on life. The big bonus is that it's easy to work.

Silt. Halfway between sand and clay in texture but, when wet, it packs down and drains badly just like clay. It also supports the same range of plants.

Chalk. Normally light in color, it does actually look a bit sick. There are often lumps of chalk in it and water drains quickly, taking the nutrients with it. The topsoil is frequently a thin covering over a rocky subsoil and a lot of plants just don't like it. Always alkaline – see page 25.

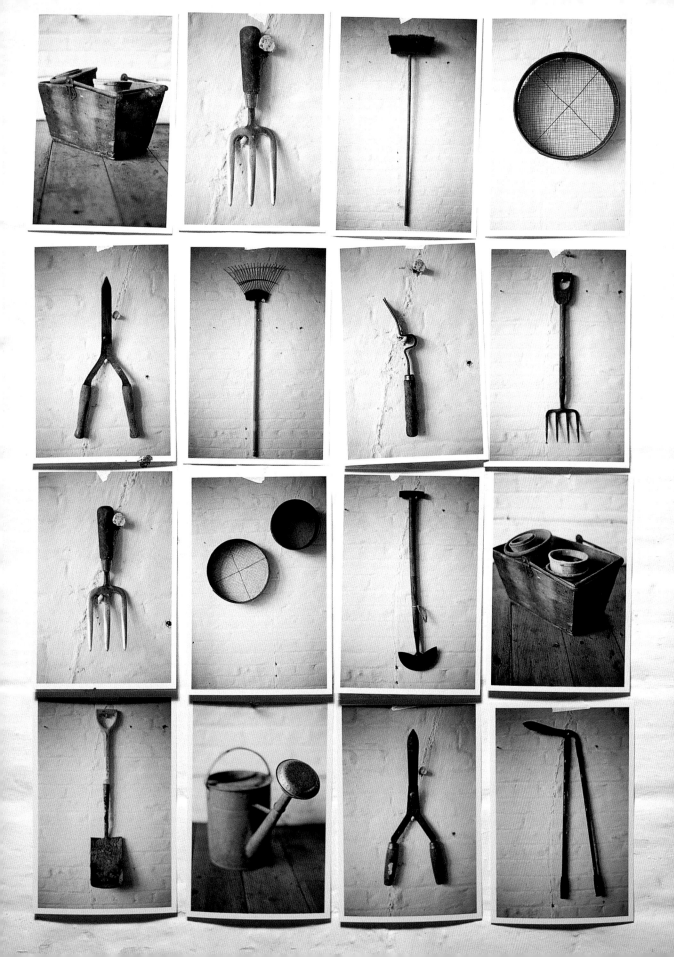

Peat. Dark, moisture-retentive and more common in a bog than in a garden. Although often fertile, peat soils do need certain nutrients added. Nearly always acid – see below.

The main thing is – don't panic. Whatever soil you have, you can improve it in a number of ways, all of which are covered in the *Compost* section. You may need to keep turning to *Compost* to check on matters earthy. Get used to doing this and, above all, don't be put off by words like lime, acid, alkaline and nitrogen. It is all infinitely manageable.

Acid and alkaline

Lots of people don't bother testing the soil and you certainly don't have to. But if you know what sort you've got, you're in a better position to improve it – and everything you grow will grow quicker and better.

The pH scale measures acidity and alkalinity from 1 to 14. The lower the number the more acid the soil; the higher the number the more alkaline; 7 is neutral. Soils range from about 3.5 to 8.5 and their pH affects what lives in them and what nutrients are available to the plants. Most plants prefer a range of 6.3 to 6.8, just fractionally on the acid side of neutral, although there are certain plants that prefer very acid or alkaline conditions.

Most of the plants covered in this book will grow happily in a normal pH range, in other words not really alkaline or really acidic.

Rhododendrons, azaleas, camellias, flame vine and lupines are all typical acid-lovers; Chinese plumbago, sea holly and potentilla will all grow in chalky soil.

1. There are two approaches to testing your soil.

   You can go out and buy – very cheaply – a soil-testing kit from a garden center and follow the instructions. This will measure the pH of your soil very precisely in a litmus sort of way. Test the soil in different parts of the garden and take an average because results do tend to vary.

   or

2. You can just look around you and see what sort of things grow well in the area. You may live on Long Island and know already that your soil is very sandy. If in doubt – buy a kit or ask someone.

   Now, whatever your results, *don't try to dramatically change the pH of the soil*, just plant the right plants. If you try to alter the pH you are embarking on a never-ending project, constantly adding and working in loads of manure. However, don't despair. Slight adjustments can be made to accommodate your favorite plants and these are covered later in *Compost*.

What you don't want

Awful plants must go at once, but be careful. Trees can be protected by local ordinances. Chopping down, or even a bit of pruning, can get you into serious trouble and the resulting fines can be huge. If you've got a tree that looks important, check with your local authority.

Strawberry tree

Call your local planning department or environmental protection agency. You may need to make a written application before you start work but they'll let you know the procedure.

So – things must go or be reduced in size if they are:

Ugly
Screening a nice view
Making too much shade
Unsuitable for your scheme, i.e. wrong color (see *Structure and Color*)
Diseased or dead
In the way
Just too damned big

Things should stay if they are:

Nice to look at – obviously
Providing desired shade
Eminently suitable
A present from your mother

Unless you're really unlucky there will be a few things that you'll want to keep. A tree, a climber, a path or an arbor. Perhaps they'll need pruning or cleaning up – maybe the lawn can be reshaped to become more interesting – but at least you've got something to work with. If you're left with some established trees and shrubs then your new-look garden will have a head start.

Too much work? This may be a good time to get someone else in to do the hard labor. A professional can advise you on what to keep and what to remove and they can do it all a lot faster than you could. That leaves you with all the nice parts and none of that garbage where you get cut to ribbons by holly bushes and step on rusty nails.

Know your limits

Have a good look at the boundaries of your garden – the fences and walls. If they're falling down all over the place then now is the time to fix them up. It's pretty easy and extremely worthwhile. If you've cleared a load of stuff and you're waiting for new plants to grow you could be staring at a broken-down old fence for some time. Obviously whole panels and posts can be replaced but it's often quite enough to patch up with a few pieces of wood, some nails and, most importantly, a good wood stain and preservative. In the past they must have been produced by Henry Ford – you could have any color you wanted as long as it was brown. Things have changed a bit now and, apart from an extensive range of browns, you can choose from many other colors including blues and greens.

If you're planting a climber against the house or any other painted wall you should consider giving the wall a quick coat of paint now because it won't be too easy once it's covered in clematis. Contrary to popular belief, climbers generally don't damage walls unless they are already in a very poor condition. Ivy and Virginia creeper, for example, actually protect brickwork – but be careful: vines can damage wood shingles and clapboards, and they can break into your attic if allowed to run riot over the roof.

Access

Before you embark on an ambitious project like cutting down a 50-foot tree or digging a hole for a lake, consider your access. This could dramatically influence the work you decide to do. What if everything has to be carried through the house or you need to get a backhoe through the side gate?

What you'll need

Tools

There's obviously plenty of choice but you really get what you pay for. Stainless-steel forks, spades and hoes are often better made and last longer than cheaper stuff. A decent pair of pruning shears is probably your most important investment; buy a good set and they'll literally last you a lifetime, unless you lose them, which is what I did.

A good pair of garden shears is essential for trimming hedges or snipping back lavender, and you'll need a set of long-handled pruners for thicker branches. Heavier work can be done with a pruning saw. A clean cut is important so keep them all sharp.

For watering, an outside faucet is your most important asset. Get a hose with a trigger nozzle and a watering can with a rose for more delicate tasks. For more delicate jobs like planting bulbs or transplanting seedlings, a hand trowel and a small weeding fork might be useful.

Lots of plants can cause nasty skin irritations, but not everyone is affected. Long sleeves and gloves will protect you and keep your hands clean, and you'll appreciate a good pair of boots if you need to do any heavy digging.

If you have a lawn you'll obviously need a mower; one with a roller if you want stripes. Long-handled shears, a half-moon edger or even an old bread knife will keep the edges neat, and for tidying up you'll need a leaf rake and a stiff broom.

But all this aside– you can do just about everything with a spade, fork, some pruners and a rake.

Money

This is the big one. How deep are your pockets? Deciding on a budget is quite important at this stage. It also makes sense to carry out large amounts of work in the garden at the beginning because it's more economical than traipsing off to the garden center every weekend and spending another hundred bucks. Buying in bulk is by far the best, because you can often negotiate discounts and it makes it easier to plan the whole layout.

Unfortunately, the garden is always last – after the kitchen and the bathroom. This doesn't make sense. If you plant the garden first then it will have time to establish and mature while you're doing everything inside, and it'll be cheaper. Go on, be different – do the garden first.

structure and color

Remember, some of the best gardens have been created by rank amateurs. It's easy for an experienced gardener to become a specimen snob and create some sort of plant zoo where the overall effect can be surprisingly dull. It's also worth bearing in mind that no matter how brilliantly the garden is designed, with paths and patios and pools, it is the plants that make it. A garden without any expensive landscape features can be tremendously successful as long as the planting is right.

It's been written a thousand times before but it's true: a garden is just an outdoor room and probably the largest one in your house. Most people find it easy to decorate the interior of their homes even if they just buy off-the-shelf style from Ikea; but for some reason that confidence is lost as soon as they step outside. The truth is that the same principles can be applied and the technicalities of gardening can be overcome later. A garden should have a personality and it should be a reflection of your own, just as your living room is.

There are no rights or wrongs, but at this stage you need to come up with a theme or direction; it doesn't matter if it evolves during conception or as you put it together, but your garden will be more successful if you fix on some sort of design or overall effect. This chapter will help you to do this. Your chosen scheme – formal or informal, modern or traditional – should ideally unify the garden as a whole. Structure and unity of design are important too.

The future. How long will you stay living in your home? Obviously you can't predict a lottery win, a career change or marriage to a wealthy heiress, but it's worth getting out your crystal ball. What you decide to plant will be affected by the answer to this question. It may be only a few years, in which case I recommend you turn to the *Ballistic* plants section. If it's a bit longer, long enough to see changes of government and maybe even a few kids, then perhaps you can afford to be a little more patient with what you grow. You could plant a strawberry tree that won't look good for years but is worth every minute of waiting. Even if you do decide to stay for only a short time, remember two things: first, I bet you stay longer than you think; and second, plant something for the future. So what if you won't live there long enough to appreciate it? You'll probably take the curtains and rugs when you go, so why not leave a decent tree?

Plant associations

No, not something to join when you're really into gardening. It's a visual thing. You can do this anywhere that there are plants – in the countryside, in the park or your mom's garden. Look at a group of plants together, never as individuals. See how one contrasts with another, making it stand out, one complementing the other in a self-promotion contest. It may be leaf shape, flower color or the overall shape of the plant that causes this juxtaposition to be so important. A common mistake is to group plants of similar leaf size together; the effect is just a hazy mess. This often happens when people pay too much attention to flowers and not enough to leaves when they're buying.

A good trick of professional garden designers is to note blocks of plants that associate well together both physically and esthetically and then regurgitate them at every opportunity. It works, so why not? You can do this too just by copying ideas from existing gardens and tailoring them for your own needs. But don't try to mimic a large garden in a small plot. It's like buying a cheap toy: it never works.

Year-round interest

A garden is a movable feast and different schemes can appear and disappear as the seasons change. To get it right, flowering periods need to be taken into account and worked out. Go for plants with a long flowering season and think about when you want the garden to look its best.

I do talk about winter color later, but if you're not going to go into the garden much in the winter, why take up valuable space by planting a load of stuff just because it has pretty sticks once the leaves have dropped? Let's face it, at that time of year it's probably dark when you get home from work anyway.

Obviously the front garden needs more careful attention; you will inevitably see this just about every day. Even if your front garden is nothing more than a window box between you and the street, do yourself a favor and spruce it up whatever the time of year.

If you've established some sort of evergreen framework, you've already provided some basic year-round interest. All you need to do now is liven up the areas opposite and immediately adjacent to windows and doors. You might want to include some scented plants.

Lawn or not

If your garden is small, urban and in shade, then lose the lawn. A bit harsh maybe, but it will never look good and will probably be so small that it's a choice between buying a lawnmower and a good pair of scissors. There are many alternatives either on their own or in combinations. Paving or wood decking, gravel (a good, cheap, attractive, plant-friendly, low-maintenance option), massed ground-cover planting, or simply making the beds bigger. More of this later in the *Lawns* section but clearly you have to consider it as part of your design.

Planning a color scheme

Shake the idea from your head that color means flowers. A garden can be full of color without actually having flowers at all. Look at all the different leaves, colored stems, barks and berries. Even if foliage is used only as a foil or framework for the brighter colors of flowers, it still serves an important function and should not be forgotten.

Think about the colors of buildings, borrowed views, paving, trees and fences – you may want to take these into account. Remember that you can paint things and introduce artificial color. A word of warning though: a beautiful old brick wall can't be un-painted so think carefully before you open the can.

As I said before, never view plants in isolation as one color influences another. So don't just think of neighboring plants or even adjoining flower beds but think how whole areas will look next to each other.

If your garden is large enough, use different color schemes in different areas. Don't overdo it though, or the whole thing will become too busy.

In a small garden a single color scheme can become boring quite quickly. Give yourself room to maneuver by using green as a backdrop and adding a range of carefully combined colors.

Massing drifts of seasonal color into different areas is more dramatic than diluting it throughout the whole garden and losing the impact.

Be careful about putting strongly colored, contrasting foliages together unless you're setting out to make a definite point. Purple, blue and yellow leaves together are like blond hair and black eyebrows, and just never look quite right. In nature plants evolve and adapt to suit their habitat and the outcome is a blend of plants that look comfortable together.

Green. Green is a restful color and can be used as a framework – particularly in a small garden – or as a scheme in its own right. Concentrate on contrasting leaf shape, size, color and texture. In many ways this is the easiest color to work with because mistakes are fewer and harder to make. The greater the contrast, the more successful the effect. A large-leaved Japanese aralia looks wonderful next to a fine-leaved bamboo. Introduce variegated leaves, although use sparingly and never next to each other. Green flowers such as hellebores and euphorbias are sophisticated, beautiful plants and prove very useful. If it's a foliage garden you want, other colors can be included to lift the green – for example, the black leaves of lilyturf or the purple of the smoke bush.

Red and orange. Use stimulating reds and oranges, coppers and golds. These strong, sometimes brash colors jump out at you and retain a sharp outline even as you move away from them, thus distorting perspective. So beware – they can make a small garden seem even smaller especially if planted at the end, clearly defining the boundary.

It's important to get the whole range, from the intense red of Crocosmia 'Lucifer', through the orange of the lily 'Enchantment' to the harsh yellow of yarrow and coneflowers. These light, bright, warm colors are shown at their best among a framework of green. Summer is the best time for a hot border. Not only is it more likely to harmonize with the weather but the choice of suitable plants is much greater.

Green hellebore

Delphinium

Dogwood

Pale blue and lavender. Blues become almost luminous and shining in the twilight – particularly useful if you're likely to be an evening garden-user. Unlike hot colors these tend to blur boundaries, melting into the distance and creating an illusion of space. Choose from the many blues of California lilac, exotic African lilies, carpets of catmint, campanula and Chinese plumbago. Blend these with lavender, hydrangeas, osteospermum and geranium and you can't go wrong.

Yellow flowers and golden foliage. Yellow attracts attention. It draws the eye before any other color and can be welcoming, exciting and uplifting – so throw out the Lithium and the Prozac, ditch the blues and get yellow instead. Primroses, daffodils and euphorbias are the heralds of spring and broom, potentilla and daylilies boldly announce the arrival of summer. For a gleaming garden, mix with golden and yellow-variegated foliages like mock orange, black locust, bamboos and plantain lilies. Be careful though, because you could create an unnatural feel. These colors are frequently sun lovers but if the right plants are chosen, they can be used to brighten a dull, shady corner. Try Bowles' golden grass, leopard's bane, Japanese laurel and lady's mantle.

White, silver and blue. A truly white border can be fairly dull, but mix in the silver foliage of wormwood and *Convolvulus cneorum* with the blue of delphinium, monkshood and sea holly, and you've got a winner. As flowers bloom and fade this combination can be both stimulating and restful and it can easily be achieved in a small sunny spot. Go one step further and add yellow, but nothing too harsh.

Purple, dark blue and black. Don't overdo this or you'll create something somber and funereal and you'll be reaching for your favorite Wagner CD and a length of rope. The quest to produce truly black tulips and violets is an obsession for many and there are some particularly dark flowers commonly available now; for example, very deep blue and purple varieties of monkshood and delphinium. Almost black foliage is provided by lilyturf and rich purple by Japanese maples, smoke bush, ligularia and *Pittosporum tenuifolium* 'Purpureum.' Silvery-grey-leaved plants can break up the dark swathes and cheer the whole thing up.

Winter color. As I've already said, your garden may well be a bit of a no-go zone at this time of year so it might not even bother you. Attempting a winter color scheme is a risky business because success will always be at the expense of the summer, which is when you'll appreciate your garden most. In a small garden you need plants with several attributes, such as rowan, which provides flowers in spring, rich autumn colors and bright berries in winter. Another winner is dogwood – variegated foliage in summer and brilliant red stems in winter. Evergreen trees and shrubs are essential. The bluey-green leaves of eucalyptus and the ornamental barks of birches and the paperbark maple do the job.

Planting themes

Tropical. Making a "tropical" garden is relatively simple, even in a chilly climate. You can create a lush, verdant oasis using totally hardy plants with bold green foliage such as Japanese aralia and Chinese rhubarb. A hardy Japanese banana and a Chusan fan palm bolster the illusion and an overhead canopy of leaves to provide shade can be supplied by the black locust. Introduce color with some "tropical" flowers: arum lilies, canna and iris.

Mediterranean. A fairly sunny spot is ideal for groupings of robust pencil conifers such as *Cupressus sempervirens* 'Stricta,' some cabbage palms, euphorbias and perhaps the odd fan palm. Swap your lawn for gravel, put some red geraniums in pots, paint the trellis blue. Plant plenty of herbs and free-flowering plants to self-seed in the gravel – mullein, poppies and wormwood are perfect – and you won't want to go on vacation at all.

Romantic. Plants can create moods. A shady seat beneath a weeping birch, plenty of ferns, delphiniums and lupines, a carpet of bluebells and the perfume of honeysuckle will have you crooning before you can say compost. A large lawn or paved area is a bit of a passion killer, so use plants to enclose spaces and make them more intimate. Think about arbors and corners covered in climbers.

Contemporary. Try using architectural plants like bamboo, New Zealand flax and pineapple flower. Concentrate on dramatic forms and foliage with strong shapes and bright colors and link the plantings directly to architectural elements of the building by color or shape. Go for clean lines. Less is more.

Formal. As a basic rule, start near the building with geometric planting areas and introduce curves and softer shapes as you move down the garden, allowing nature more of a say. Dwarf box hedging and clipped topiary specimens can immediately age the garden by a couple of centuries.

Games. If you like to kick a football around, choose the right plants: some sturdy shrubs like Japanese laurel and viburnum and a couple of trees for goalposts. Avoid delicate flowers and thorny shrubs like barberry or there'll be tears before bedtime.

Hide and seek

Views and viewpoints. Borrowing views from next door and beyond is an important part of any planting design. Be sure to look outside your own fences and see if there's anything you'd like to incorporate into your garden. Perhaps you want to see the spectacular autumn foliage of a liquid gum tree or the ornamental façade of the neighboring school. When designing your planting you can frame these views – or, of course, you may want to blank out something hideous.

Privacy. As I said before, seclusion and privacy are particularly important in an urban garden. The neighbors are probably a bit closer than you'd wish and creating a sanctuary among all the chaos outside is high on your list. First identify the main overlooking windows and intrusive views and then the areas of your garden that you'll most frequently use – the patio, a seating area, the sun porch. Now simply block out the sight lines with strategically placed trees and thick shrubbery. Move them around a bit before you plant them to make sure they're in exactly the right place. Be careful not to plant trees too close to a building (especially birch and eucalyptus); you may need to substitute with trellis and climbers to get the necessary height.

Don't be tempted to plant formal hedges, particularly conifers, unless they are specifically in keeping with the design or architectural style of your house. Instead, use a mixed hedge of all evergreen shrubs. Speed is probably important too, so select well. Laurels, photinias and pittosporums are always a good choice. To get a little extra privacy try erecting trellises on your existing walls and fences – but go too high, and you'll make yourself a cage. It's not nice to fix things to your neighbor's fence without permission – so if you haven't fallen out yet, now is your chance. Good, fast, value-for-money climbers for trellises are *Clematis montana*, jasmine and ornamental vines.

Focal points. Focal points or areas can be created by single plants or groups of plants at the end of a vista, opposite a doorway or window. You can create a vista by drawing the eye through a narrowing path of planting or landscape features such as paths and arbors. The focal point may even be a borrowed view or something you've created – an urn or sculpture or some vibrant planting against a dull foil of evergreens. Remember bright, warm colors leap out at you and draw the eye well, making a good focal point.

Seating areas with benches can also serve as focal points or simply as surprise features within the garden. It is human nature to sit with your back against something so some trellis or a wall of planting is essential. Obviously it's wise to avoid thorny plants such as barberry but it is good to use scented plants such as Mexican orange blossom and fragrant viburnum. Any overhead timbers can be clothed in perfumed climbers like jasmine and honeysuckle.

Mystery. A few rules. Hide those fences and boundaries. Even in a very small garden this will create an illusion of space. Not being able to see exactly where the garden ends is essential and it's a simple trick. Cover them in climbers and hide them with shrubs and perennials. Draw the eye away to other things in a "Quick, look at that tree!" kind of way. It's sleight of hand. Of course it's a transparent trick but it works time and time again, even for whoever did the planting. People are easily fooled.

Disrupt the view so the entire garden can't be seen at once. It's the same trick really but what you want to do here is to create a bit of mystery and intrigue. Break up the garden with planting, leaving tantalizing glimpses of what's to come, so that you actually have to walk around the shrub to see what's going on, even though you already know.

Black lilyturf

A door that doesn't lead anywhere can be set into a wall, or a cleverly positioned mirror can be put among the planting to create a false perspective or an illusion of space. Try these tricks out before you actually build them permanently because they may need moving around to achieve the desired effect. If you can accommodate some existing planting they will seem real much sooner.

Cut the work

A short cut to a low-maintenance garden is to have a balance within it: a mix of evergreen and deciduous, shrub and perennial (see *Glossary* on page 56).

Avoid single-species flower beds – for example, one full of just roses – and maximize space by under-planting clean-stemmed plants with ground-cover plants that smother weeds and look good. Choosing the correct ground cover is essential; the cranesbill *Geranium macrorrhizum* is one of the best.

Get rid of bare soil as soon as possible – mulch, (see page 47) will help, but this may hinder self-seeders. Make sure that within your design you choose things that will eventually close together and all but eliminate weeding. This is easier than you think and just depends on plant selection. The extra effort now could save you hours of work every week.

Avoid high-maintenance plants. These are things that catch diseases and need spraying and lots of reg-ular pruning: hybrid tea roses are a good example.

Remember that evergreen plants don't lose their leaves and therefore don't make as much mess as deciduous plants. This is particularly relevant when selecting trees.

Planting structure

When planting it's helpful to think of the structure of the garden as being in three tiers or layers. Each layer has a separate function but cannot stand alone. Imagine each "layer" of plants drawn on transparent acetate sheets. One may be overlaid onto the next to create the finished effect. There are no hard and fast rules for which plants fall into which layer. These are only guidelines and as long as you wander around, in or near them, then you're on the right track.

1. Framework

Having already established what to keep and what to remove, you will probably be left with a few mature plants and trees, possibly a bit of lawn, and some bare beds. It is unlikely that you will have a clean canvas on which to work unless you have a brand-new house.

The first step is to create a framework of planting. This dictates the shape and ultimate personality of your garden. It will include trees and large shrubs. The trees will be used to screen neighboring buildings and views, create shade, and add a third dimension to the garden. The large shrubs perform the same function on a smaller scale and in a very small garden can be used as an alternative to trees.

Crocosmia

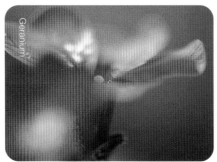

Geranium

Euphorbia

2. Middle Tier

The majority of your planting will probably fall into this category: medium-sized shrubs and perennials (see *Glossary* on page 56) providing color and interest, determining and strengthening your chosen design. Select these to associate well together and fit the available space. As a very basic guide, the tall ones go at the back and the low ones at the front; however, don't be afraid to buck this trend. Try planting something tall at the front: a bronze fennel for example can create an interesting focal point and provide a welcome relief from rows of plants like spectators at a tennis match. An architectural plant like New Zealand flax creates punctuation, the planting beyond becoming a new and interesting phrase.

Planting in groups creates a more dramatic, bold effect and breaks up the monotony of even spots of color and foliage – but don't put everything in blocks. Odd numbers of plants should always be used; this is a basic rule of design (apart from formal symmetry). Put two anythings together. Now add a third. Much better.

3. Lower Ground

This is basically everything else. Ground cover to prevent weeds, infill planting for gaps. Many new plantings are let down at the end by the virtual exclusion of this stage. It's not just the icing on the cake, it's an integral element. It comes last in the thought process and yet needs to be at the forefront of the mind throughout the planning stage. Get this right and it really lifts the planting.

What you plant will obviously be dictated by your overall garden plan. These plants are often smaller but can link everything else together or provide splashes of unexpected color.

Time

The problem is that once you've done all the back-breaking digging, bought the plants and spent all your cash, you want to see some results. Sorry, but you've got to wait. Those tiny plants from the garden center look even smaller now that they're in the ground and there seems to be bare earth everywhere.

There are ways to beat this: planting groups rather than individuals; and buying a couple of large plants, which will instantly mature your garden. Sow self-seeders (see *Grow Your Own*), which will fill the gaps each year with annuals and biennials but still allow the other plants to develop.

compost, manure and mulch

Improving your soil

Compost, manure and mulch might not sound overly romantic – rather the opposite – but believe me, once you've got a working idea of matters earthy, you're all set. Plants need to have a balanced diet of the right kind of foods just as we do. So, first off we need to demystify soil improvers: bulky organic matter and fertilizers. Then we can work out when and how to use them and improve the particular soil you have.

A healthy soil is the basis of all good gardening, and organic practices absolutely depend upon it. The tenet of organic gardening is to feed the soil rather than the plants. It is the soil that supports all the life. So this is what we're interested in here – improving the structure and fertility of the soil. Nutrients can be provided by bulky organic matter, also known as soil improvers, and by more concentrated and specific fertilizers.

It can be as simple as throwing some fertilizer onto the ground. But the plant must be able to use the nutrients we supply, and in order to do this, the structure of the soil must be fairly good.

Bulky organic matter

Virtually all gardening tomes refer to "bulky organic matter" – but what is it? Basically it's bulky as opposed to concentrated granules or liquids; it's organic because it's a product of nature; and finally, it's matter because it's stuff, and it really does matter. It's crazy not to use it in the garden.

It opens up the soil, improves drainage and eases the way for root growth. It helps overdrained soil retain water and therefore nutrients. Organic matter can be provided by any of the following things. They all perform more or less the same function, though they supply different ranges of nutrients. The best and simplest way to use them is to fork them into the surface layer of the soil.

Compost
Compost is basically any rotted-down organic matter. You can make it yourself – throw a load of old garbage in at one end, and months later you take out wonderful crumbly compost at the other. Organic matter means grass cuttings, bits of plants, leaves and even household waste; we'll go into the details later (see page 52). You can also buy compost, but making it is the perfect way of recycling garden waste. With the help of bacteria and a bit of time, the rotted material returns valuable nitrogen (the most basic nutrient, and particularly good for general growth) to the soil. As stuff decomposes, it actually uses nitrogen, so it needs to finish "composting" before you apply it to the soil. Then it puts the nitrogen back in.

Animal manures
Animal manure is the best and most compact source of organic matter for your garden, but it's harder to come by. Horse manure is the easiest to get hold of in or near urban areas, from riding stables. Be careful, though. If the horses' bedding is straw, that's fine, but if it's wood shavings, it's not, as these can harbor plant diseases. Ideally

the manure should be put on the compost heap or left to rot for a couple of months. You can put it directly onto the beds but it may use up nitrogen from the soil as it rots, and if put directly around plants it can cause scorching. It contains all the major nutrients and trace elements (see page 48). You can use other animal manures such as cow or chicken if you know of a source. Dried forms are available from garden centers.

Alternatives

Spent mushroom compost, which you can get from some garden centers, is alkaline and can therefore be used to raise the pH, so don't use it around acid-loving plants. It's a good substitute for manure and is a good conditioner for heavy clay soils, but it can scorch plants if put directly up against them, and it may contain chemical residues.

Seaweed can be bought or picked up at the beach. It improves soil structure and is rich in trace elements. Hose off the salt and dig it straight into the soil or throw it on the compost heap.

Composted bark is often sold as a soil improver – but beware. Unrotted bark has no nutrient value and even if used on the surface as a mulch it actually takes nitrogen from the soil as it decomposes.

Green manure

This is a way of introducing nutrients and organic matter directly to a patch of bare ground that you may want to cultivate in the future. The idea is to sow a crop that smothers and discourages weeds and can then be dug straight into the ground in as little as six weeks from start to finish. There's no composting involved and the ground is automatically ready for planting. Sow fava beans in late summer or autumn. The plants will grow through the winter and you get an edible crop into the bargain. When you're ready to use the ground, cut them down, let them wilt for a few days and dig them in about 6 inches deep. Other suitable plants are lupines, mustard and vetches.

Mulches

A mulch can basically be anything that you spread over the soil surface around the plants. It will keep the soil warm and moist and therefore promote root growth and prevent drought, making for a happier, healthier plant. It's what happens in nature when a layer of leaf mold builds up on the woodland floor. It protects roots from frosts and ultimately fertilizes the soil. It's a really good idea to put a mulch down after planting because it helps establishment and reduces the amount of watering you have to do. A thick layer of mulch will stop weeds from growing but you must weed the ground first, otherwise troublesome individuals like dandelion, couch grass and bindweed will grow through (see *Maintenance*). Compost is a double-action mulch because it protects and feeds at the same time.

Ideally, mulches are not a one-time thing. An annual dose is good but unlikely. Once every couple of years is fine – but one application is better than nothing.

Any bulky organic matter can be used as long as you follow a few rules.

— Keep it away from plant stems to prevent them from rotting.

— Apply organic mulch between 2 and 4 inches deep or it's a waste of time.

— Unrotted matter will remove nitrogen from the soil so be prepared to add supplementary fertilizers.

— Remove all weeds first, especially perennials, or they'll grow through.

Anything can be used as a mulch but esthetics are important here. Organic gardeners are always ranting on about using old carpet, but it's not very pretty, is it? Where do you get old carpet from anyway? Black polyethylene sheeting from the garden center is good. You can cut it to fit around established plants or plant new ones through it by making a slit. Cover it with an organic mulch, even an unrotted one, and once it has decomposed, whip out the plastic and fork the organic mulch in to improve the texture of the soil. You can also use newspaper and then cover it with bark. Once it's decomposed, the whole thing can just be turned into the soil. People often use cocoa shells because they smell nice, but they're expensive and they dry up and blow away. Ornamental bark chips, especially the composted type, are quite a good option because they're cheap and they look good.

One word of warning though. I write later in *Grow Your Own* about self-seeders being one of the most satisfying ways of propagating – and they are. But they're not all that compatible with mulches, because just as a mulch will keep weeds out, it can also defeat new seedlings from settling in.

In short – if in doubt, mulch. There are many more pros than cons and as long as it's well rotted, you can't really go wrong.

Organic fertilizers

The big three fertilizers are nitrogen for healthy leaves, phosphorus (phosphates) for roots, and potassium (potash) for flowers and fruit. A range of trace elements including magnesium, sulfur and iron help with all the other needs.

If you do decide to use fertilizers as a matter of course, simply apply a general fertilizer like fish, blood and bonemeal in spring and again in summer. If you have only one fertilizer on your shelf, this is the one to have. Always wear gloves when handling fertilizers. Follow the directions on the package, but normally a couple of handfuls per square yard is a good guide. Scratch it into the soil surface with the prongs of a fork or rake it in.

For ardent vegetarians who may shy away from these animal byproducts, a better, although more expensive, alternative is dried seaweed meal. It's got a more balanced range of nutrients because it also contains all the trace elements. Liquid seaweed will correct soil deficiency very quickly and allegedly protects plants against fungus and frost.

Applying liquid feeds to dry ground will damage the roots of plants so water thoroughly first.

If you've composted and manured, you may have already provided enough nutrients and you may not need to add extra fertilizers at all, unless the soil is really bad.

Synthetic fertilizers can harm the soil, whereas organic ones actually help the microorganisms essential to the food chain; so don't cheat and add the wrong thing.

It may be tempting to go fertilizer crazy but don't get carried away. With any fertilizer there is a danger of overdose, which can cause poor plant health and even death.

Nutrient deficiencies

You may still encounter problems: for example, sick-looking plants that don't seem to be diseased. If a plant seems scrawny and the leaves, particularly the older ones, are discolored, the problem could be a nutrient deficiency.

You might have to delve a little deeper and identify the deficiency.

Here's a quick guide:

— Leaves turn yellow, plants are stunted: Nitrogen deficiency. Add dried blood.

— Older leaves turn a sort of bluish-green and root growth is poor: Phosphorus deficiency. Apply bonemeal.

— Small flowers and fruit, and leaves turn yellow around the edge: Potassium deficiency. Apply potash.

— Older leaves turn yellow or silvery-yellow between the veins: Magnesium deficiency. Apply seaweed meal.

— Younger leaves turn yellow between the veins. Iron deficiency: Apply seaweed meal.

Acid or alkaline made easy

As we've already seen in *What You've Got,* you can discover the pH of the soil by either testing or looking over your fence. An acid soil, with a pH less than 7.0, supports a greater range of plants than a chalky, alkaline soil. If you want to grow acid-loving plants like camellia and rhododendron, and your garden is a superalkaline solid layer of chalk, then use a raised bed (a specially constructed bed, encased with brick or wood and filled with the soil of your choice) or containers that you can fill with acid soil or peat moss compost.

To make the soil more alkaline, fork in spent mushroom compost or lime, which is basically a bag of chalk dust bought from a garden center. Scatter it on the soil and fork it in. For specific plants that need more alkaline soil, add lime locally. Thyme benefits from this even in a neutral soil. To make the soil more acid, a regular dose of organic matter (compost or manure) should do the trick, supplemented with liquid seaweed or chelated iron.

Your particular soil needs

If a garden has been worked in the past and then neglected for a period, the chances are that the structure and fertility of the soil will not be too far wrong. On the other hand, if it's been uncultivated for years or is a brand-new garden, it's likely to need improvement. You *may* get away without doing much to it apart from adding a bit of fertilizer, but if in doubt, remember that all soils benefit from the addition of bulky organic matter such as well-rotted compost or manure.

Clay. If your clay is very heavy, it can take a few years to improve it; but once you've done so, it can be a good soil to have. Dig it when it's not too wet or too dry, preferably in autumn, and then let it get broken up by frosts. Add plenty of bulky organic matter to make it lighter and easier to work. Adding sand improves drainage and makes it lighter, as does lime, but watch your pH levels.

Sand. Digging is not so important. Sandy soils dry out fast, so organic mulching cuts down evaporation and improves soil structure as it rots. Because the rain washes nutrients out of sand so fast, choose your plants to maintain a protective covering of foliage, especially in the winter, and fork bulky organic matter into the top layer as often as possible.

Silt. Don't walk on silt when it's wet enough to stick to your shoes, because that will ruin the structure. Otherwise treat as for a clay soil with plenty of organic matter.

Chalk. The topsoil is often shallow but you can dig it whenever you want to. Nutrients are washed out very quickly so it's a hungry soil. Lots of organic stuff slows down the drainage and helps the soil hang on to the nutrients for longer. It may also make the soil less alkaline and increase the range of plants that you can grow. Fertilizers will also be needed. Mulching is important to cut down evaporation, and growing a green manure, or other plants that cover the surface, is hugely important to stop the rain washing the goodness away.

Peat. Peaty soils are easy to cultivate. They can support a wide range of plants, but lime may need to be added for certain vegetables. Peat will probably be low in nutrients and need fertilizing. Very peaty soils are difficult to rehydrate if they dry out, but others can become waterlogged, so some sort of drainage system may be needed.

Making a compost heap

A steaming heap of compost is a blissful sight in winter, and it's the perfect and organic way of reusing kitchen and garden waste. You can either go and buy a compost bin from a garden center or make something yourself.

This can be a bit Rube Goldberg-like, and there are many different ways of putting one together, so do a bit of investigating. But whether you get clever with railroad ties, wood pallets or wire fence, the basic principle is a container with a cover to keep it warm. It can be as simple as a black garbage bag, tied up at the top. Shove a fork through in a few places for ventilation and leave it for a year or so. Whatever – it needs a bit of air and the occasional shuffle so it doesn't get compacted, or you'll end up with grassy slime, which is useless. The bag technique is especially good for leaves.

People tend to throw all sorts of things onto compost heaps, including old leather shoes, on the basis that they're organic. In theory, if it used to be alive you can use it (as long as you chop it up small enough) but in reality this isn't quite true.

Don't compost anything that's diseased or pest-ridden. Take it to the dump. Sticks, bits of woody plants and evergreen leaves take ages to rot, but if you must use them, chop them up very small or use a shredder. Nasty weeds like bittersweet, dandelion, bindweed and couch grass will spread rapidly if you put even little bits of root into the compost. Uncooked kitchen garbage is fine but animal products attract mice and rats. Tea bags, coffee grounds, orange peel, eggshells and all that sort of stuff is great.

If you inherit a compost heap with the garden, then have a good poke around in it. Remove sticks, roots, weeds and other things that quite clearly aren't rotting. Because you won't know the pedigree of the heap, experiment by using a little at a time in case it's full of weeds.

Buying compost

The sort of compost you'll be producing in your heap will be more than adequate for forking into the beds, using as a mulch or for new plantings, but there may come a time when you have to buy some. When you've only just started your heap or you're planting in containers, you'll need to get something more convenient. And if you have a small garden without a lawn, you may not produce enough of your own compost. Garden centers sell it for every purpose: potting compost, leaf mold compost for acid-loving plants, seed compost and so on. The best bet is to go for an organic general-purpose compost that is just that. Watch out though: avoid peat and peat-based composts. The draining of ancient wetlands to get this peat has destroyed important habitats forever. Not only that, but peat gets waterlogged or dries out completely – so it's not all that great anyway.

the plants

Every weekend happy gardeners pour out of garden centers having spent hundreds of dollars on wonderful new plants. But almost immediately, those plants are on their way to a long, slow death. The reason for this is simple: success can only be guaranteed if you choose the right plant for the right place. The plants selected here are generally sturdy, hardy and reliable, with a lengthy period of interest whether their thing is flowers, berries, leaves or whatever. There is, however, the occasional exception: some particularly striking or unique plants are included because I deem them worthy of a bit of extra trouble. You may also find some old favorites missing: forsythia, buddleja and red tulips, for example. You'll know forsythia. Suburbia in spring is drenched in bright, sordid yellow flowers glaring at you. We've reached forsythia saturation point and there are alternatives – so that's out and other more desirable plants are in.

If you follow these simple guidelines for plant selection and planting, you will have a new garden that will look fantastic and, once established, will thrive on neglect. It won't give up and die just because you were busy at work during that particular spring. You'll find yourself relaxing in a deck chair with a nice glass of wine while your neighbor gets all anxious with his lawnmower. Gardening's as much about being as it is about doing.

Within many of the sections, the listed plants are mainly a broad mix of shrubs and perennials providing a wide range of colors, shapes and textures. And so in most cases it would be possible, though not essential, to select all the plants from one section to create a fine spread over quite a long period. I have recommended the ideal growing conditions and maintenance for each plant.

There are many different plants featured in other parts of the book. *Birds, Bees and Salamanders* includes a range of flowers specifically for attracting wildlife; and *Lawns* includes wildflowers and bulbs.

Glossary

Botany is a science – gardening is not. The terms below are nonscientific, user-friendly gardening terms. As a result they may seem a bit vague but that's just the way gardening is and that's why I like it.

Annual. These are normally grown from seed (sunflowers, for example) or bought in small polystyrene trays (like lobelia) and are described as bedding plants. They do everything they have to do in one year and then that's it – the frost comes and they're in the compost bin.

Biennial. These are like annuals only they take two years to get to the flowering part (one example is foxgloves). They're meant to die after two years but some of them keep going and some self-seed anyway.

Bulbs and corms. Daffodils and onions are bulbs; crocus and cyclamen are corms. The difference is botanical, but essentially they are the underground stores that send up the flowers and leaves each year. These die down in much the same way as a herbaceous perennial.

Cultivar. This is a cultivated variety, a hybrid created by clever gardeners or breeders.

Deciduous. Leaves drop off in winter.

Evergreen. The leaves stay on all year round.

Ground cover. This is not just a plant that grows low to the ground but one that actually spreads to obliterate bare soil and smother weeds.

Half hardy or frost hardy. These plants will need a bit of winter protection from the cold and wind or, if they are planted in a sheltered position, can take a chance.

In warmer areas such plants may last for years – but could then succumb during a long, hard winter.

Hardy. Will withstand normal weather conditions – whatever they are – although some may suffer some minor damage under extreme winter conditions.

Panicles and racemes. These are words to describe large blooms, like those of wisteria, that are actually made up of a number of small individual flowers.

Perennial. This is anything that comes up year after year, but some are short-lived. The term usually applies to a non-woody-stemmed plant which dies down in winter and sends up new shoots in spring. This is a herbaceous perennial. Just to confuse things, some perennials are evergreen, but I wouldn't worry too much about that.

Self-seeders. These are the best annuals and biennials. Collect some seeds from a friend's garden or spend a few bucks on some packets. Sow as directed in the first year and then after that, as long as they are happy, they get on with it themselves, coming up year after year in the form of new seedlings *ad infinitum*.

Shrub. A plant with a woody framework of stems. May be deciduous or evergreen. Size is not important – can be anything from a few inches to many feet high.

Synonym (or syn.). This is the former name of a plant but one by which it's often still known, especially in garden centers or nurseries.

Tender. Basically, the plants won't survive the winter outside, and will need dragging into the house, conservatory or shed before the frosts arrive.

Tree. Without getting too technical, a tree is just like a shrub only often, but

not always, bigger and sturdier. Large shrubs can be bigger than small trees.

Variety (or var.). This is a variation on a species of plant that has occurred in nature.

Hardiness. The terms hardy, half hardy or frost hardy, and tender are particularly vague because the hardiness of a particular plant varies enormously. It depends where you live and where you plant things. To help you select the right plants for your area of the country, every plant listing in this book contains information about the zone (or zones) where it grows best. The zones shown are for the whole genus; individual species and varieties may do better in a narrower range of climates.

The USDA plant hardiness map on page 208 will show you which zone you are in. Choose plants that suit the average range of temperatures where you garden.

Latin or common

Scientific or botanical names are derived from Latin and Greek. They are listed by a generic name first, which is akin to a surname, followed by the species name, which is similar to a first name. No two species of a genus can have the same name although that species name may occur in another genus. There may also be a variety, cultivar or subspecies tacked on the end, for example *Lonicera nitida* 'Baggesen's Gold.' The scientific names are essentially a language and they can tell you a lot about a plant: flower size (*grandiflora*), country of origin (*madagascariensis*), color (*purpurea*), discoverer (*livingstonia*) and so on. What's more, they're universal. You'll already be able to recognize quite a few generic names – it doesn't take a genius to figure out what the following are: *Origanum*, *Thymus*, *Rosmarinus* and *Lavandula*. In other instances the botanical name has become the everyday term or common name – clematis, rhododendron and hydrangea to name but a few, and for this reason, you'll notice, they're not in italics. However, for the beginner there is much to learn – too much in fact. So, for this book (where there *is* a common name) we've listed that first, scientific name second.

Common names are just that – written in plain English rather than Latin – and tend to be purely descriptive (e.g., quaking grass, angels' trumpets), rather than telling you something "scientific." Quite often, too, a plant has more than one common name: the genus *Kniphofia* is known as red hot poker, poker flower and torch lily. But don't let it confuse you. If a common name attracts you, ten to one you'll like the plant.

Half the plants in my garden are bought as much for the name as for the plant itself. The naked ladies nestle against the bear's breeches, the whole being shaded by a snowy mespilus. Unfortunately this unscientific approach does have its pitfalls. The familiar red geraniums of our window boxes are actually pelargoniums. Sea holly is not holly and cabbage palms have nothing to do with vegetables.

So why put the common name first? Simple: It's the best way to start. As your interest grows, you gradually pick up knowledge both through reading books and visiting gardens, and then the Latin names become quite fun to bandy about at barbecues. And should you want to "talk plants" when abroad, everyone will know the Latin names but look blank at the English version of the common names.

Height and spread

The approximate heights and spreads at maturity are denoted in this book for each plant by *H.* and *S.* These sizes will vary enormously according to the growing conditions for each plant.

Many, particularly perennials, may reach the stated size after only a few years.

Male and female

This isn't a big deal and only affects a few of the plants in this book (see page 79), but the rub is this: many species have both male and female flowers borne on separate plants, so to get fruit and berries you'll need both sexes for pollination. Holly is the most common example and skimmia is another good one. The female has the berries, so plant one male and give him a sort of skimmia harem for the best display.

A word about soils and drainage

Fertile or rich. A fertile soil is rich in nutrients and decomposed organic matter.

Moist, well drained. For many of the listed plants a moist, well-drained soil is ideal and is a perfectly normal aspect of a half-decent soil. So, unless you've got solid clay, a layer of chalk or 100 percent sand you should be okay.

Well drained. This means that it won't ever get boggy or waterlogged like a heavy clay. The water moves freely down through the soil, which may be sandy or gritty.

Moist. This means it retains some moisture in the soil even in the summer. It wouldn't include sandy or chalky soils which dry out very fast.

Horticultural gravel or sand. These can be bought from garden centers and forked into the soil to improve drainage.

Limestone grit. This not only helps the drainage but makes the soil more alkaline as well.

Papyrus

indestructible shrubs

Without regular attention a lot of shrubs will get
straggly and misshapen, if not a little sickly, with
a poor show of flowers. I've chosen the following
shrubs because they grow at a respectable speed
and they'll survive or even thrive against all odds.
Of course they need to be planted properly in the
first place, but once that's done they just get on
with it. Most of the plants in this book will put up
with the minimum of loving, but these will tolerate
extreme neglect and even abuse. They'll tolerate a
fairly wide range of soils and you can leave them
for years without pruning or feeding. They don't
tend to get nasty diseases or pests and, apart
from veronica which doesn't ever need pruning,
you can snip bits off whenever you want. If you're
feeling particularly lazy, try planting all of these
indestructible plants together; they'll give you a
good mixture of flower colors and something
to look at throughout the year.

Note: The dimensions after every plant name
indicate height (H.) and spread (S.) at maturity.

Mexican orange blossom

Choisya ternata H. 8 feet, S. 8 feet
A very easy plant. This shrub grows quite quickly to form a solid mass of shiny evergreen leaves. Keep it to the required size by trimming bits off after flowering. The leaves are aromatic when cut or crushed and the scented, white flowers appear in spring and then normally again in summer or autumn. 'Sundance' has bright yellow leaves but rarely flowers and 'Aztec Pearl' is more graceful with much thinner leaves. They need sun or light shade in any half-decent soil. They're good in containers. Zones 8–10.

Abelia

Abelia x grandiflora 'Francis Mason' H. 5 feet, S. 6 feet
This evergreen shrub has yellow and green glossy leaves that look good on their own, but it also produces plenty of pinky-white fragrant flowers from midsummer to autumn. It'll grow in any decent soil in sun or a little bit of shade. There is a green-leaved form which is bigger. Snip straggly growth off after flowering or just let it grow. *A. chinensis* is even larger but deciduous. Zones 6–9.

Smoke bush

Cotinus coggygria H. 15 feet, S. 15 feet
A large deciduous shrub or even a small tree. You do need to give it space for it to be fully appreciated. The midgreen leaves turn yellow, orange and red in autumn, and the ethereal panicles of tiny flowers (often purply-pink) give it the name smoke bush. 'Royal Purple' obviously has purple leaves and 'Grace' turns a brilliant red in autumn. Doesn't need any pruning unless you want to control the size but cutting it well back in early spring produces larger leaves. This will grow in most soils in sun or some shade. Zones 5–8.

Euonymus

Euonymus fortunei cultivars H. 2 feet, S. indefinite
These grow in most soils in sun or light shade, and form mounds of evergeen leaves – variegated gold and white or just plain green. They don't really need any attention apart from the occasional trim. 'Emerald 'n' Gold' and 'Emerald Gaiety' are the most popular. 'Silver Queen' is a bigger and more upright plant that turns into a vigorous climber if grown against a wall. *E. japonicus* cultivars are worth looking out for. Zones 5–9.

Hebe

Hebe H. 6 inches–6 feet, S. 1 foot–6 feet
A varying bunch of evergreen flowering shrubs that are hardy or almost hardy and are happy in poor soils in sun or a bit of shade. The flowers are in spikes from white to pinks and blues and the leaves are grey-blue to purple. 'Autumn Glory' is a small shrub up to 2 feet high with dark green leaves with red edges and purple-blue flowers. 'Great Orme' is twice the size with large spikes of pink and white flowers. Between them they flower from late spring to early winter. They don't like or need pruning. Zones 8–10.

Potentilla

Potentilla fruticosa H. 3 inches–4 feet, S. 8 inches–4 feet
A deciduous shrub with small, green leaflets that flowers for ages, from late spring to midautumn. The flowers are about 1½ inches across and saucer shaped. 'Abbotswood' has white flowers, 'Red Ace' is red, 'Primrose Beauty' is primrose yellow and you can work out 'Tangerine' for yourself. They all prefer a poor or slightly fertile soil, well drained and in full sun. Lightly snip over with shears in early or midspring to keep them compact. Zones 3–8.

Shrubby lonicera

Lonicera nitida 'Baggesen's Gold' H. 6 feet, S. 6 feet
Useful for cheering up dingy areas especially in winter because the small, bright yellow leaves are evergreen. You can clip them into neat topiary shapes or leave them to their own devices. Neglected plants are easily renovated. Any soil in a bit of sun will do though the straight, green form will take some shade. They're grown for the leaves but do produce small white flowers. *L. pileata* is lower growing and makes a good ground cover. Zones 5–9.

Photinia

Photinia x fraseri 'Red Robin' H. 15 feet, S. 15 feet
This superb evergreen shrub has bright scarlet, young leaves that look great against the older, dark green ones. It makes a fairly compact bush and grows in most soils in sun or light shade. The more open and larger *P. x fraseri* has lots of small white flowers towards the end of spring and can be treated as a small tree. Pruning is needed only to restrict the size. Zones 8–9.

Laurustinus

Viburnum tinus H. 10 feet, S. 10 feet
An essential in any low-maintenance garden. This neat bush of dark evergreen leaves is covered in conspicuous heads of white flowers for ages during winter and spring. It grows fairly fast to screen things and any soil will do in sun or shade. Pruning isn't needed but you can restrict the size or strip all the lower stems bare to make it more interesting. 'Eve Price' is a cultivar with pink flower buds. Zones 8–10.

Fuchsia

Fuchsia 'Riccartonii' H. 6–10 feet, S. 3–6 feet
Possibly the best fuchsia, very hardy with lots of small scarlet and purple flowers. In frost-free places it will grow into a large bush; otherwise, cut out the dead wood to the base in spring. Other more showy cultivars like 'Mrs Popple' have bigger flowers, and the unopened buds are very good to pop. Watch out because a lot of fuchsias aren't hardy. Moist, well-drained soil in sun or light shade is best. Zones 8–10.

Other indestructible shrubs
Japanese laurel, sedge, skimmia

dependable perennials

If they're neglected for a number of years lots
of perennials will get less and less vigorous and
eventually disappear altogether, along with your
enthusiasm for gardening. Have no fear because
as long as they're in the right spot, these ones
will go on for ages without an ounce of attention.
Cutting back dead leaves and flowers helps,
but they're chores that can be ignored. If you
want you can divide them every few years but
if you don't want to, it doesn't matter. The choice
is yours. Like the shrubs in the previous section
you can plant all of these perennials to get a
long-lasting and varied display suited to a lot
of soil types and conditions. Mix them up with
the shrubs and you've got yourself an extremely
low-maintenance garden.

Yarrow

Achillea filipendulina 'Gold Plate' *H. 4 feet x S. 18 inches*
This sturdy perennial forms a clump of stems clothed in green ferny leaves and is perfect in a mixed border among shrubs and perennials. The large, convex flower heads are made up of masses of tiny, bright yellow flowers and they continue from early summer into autumn. If you like yellow this is the plant for you. Provided you give it full sun it will grow well in most soils. 'Cloth of Gold' is an even taller and equally good cultivar.

Daylily

Hemerocallis H. 30 inches x S. 30 inches
There are dozens of these clump-forming perennials with long strap-shaped leaves. The flowers range from yellows to oranges and reds but also include a few less common whites and purples. They rise above the leaves and last for only a day but flowering often continues from late spring to late summer. Pull off the dead foliage ready for spring. Divide the clumps every three to four years to retain their vigour. Moist soil in sun is best.

Lady's mantle

Alchemilla mollis H. 20 inches x S. 30 inches
You have to have this plant. From early summer to autumn the delicate greeny yellow flowers look fantastic against the soft, slightly hairy leaves. Grow it in any moist soil in sun or shade although it will put up with droughts. It's perfect for edging borders and spilling over onto paths and patios and makes an excellent ground cover. It doesn't require any special attention at all; it self-seeds freely or you can divide clumps.

Loosestrife

Lysimachia ephemerum H. 3 feet x S. 1 foot
A clump-forming perennial that sends up erect stems of grey-green leaves topped by spikes of small white flowers from early to mid-summer. *L. clethroides* is similar and equally as good. *L. punctata* is even more reliable with larger, yellow flowers and green leaves. It flowers a bit later but spreads more and is slightly more robust. Any soil will do in sun or a bit of shade.

Perennial phlox

Phlox paniculata H. 4 feet x S. 2 feet
Good value because it flowers for a long time from summer to midautumn. It forms clumps and sends out erect stalks with green leaves and clusters of fragrant flowers at the top. Flower colors range from whites to pinks and lilacs. It likes a fertile soil, preferably a bit moist, in sun or light shade. Deadheading produces more flowers. Cut the stems down in autumn and divide the plants every now and then. 'Bright Eyes' has clear pink flowers with red eyes and 'White Admiral' is as expected.

Kaffir lily

Schizostylis coccinea H. 2 feet, S. 1 foot
From southern Africa, this almost evergreen perennial is a bit of a show-off. It flowers quite late, when not much else does, from late summer to early winter. It has thin strap-shaped leaves and the flower spikes are great for cut flowers. It's ideal for most gardens in half-decent sunny soil that stays a little moist. It can be divided in spring. 'Major' has big red flowers and other cultivars are various pinks. Zones 7–9.

Stonecrop

Sedum spectabile H. 1 foot 6 inches, S. 1 foot 6 inches
A succulent perennial with fleshy grey-green leaves. In late summer it produces flat heads of small, pink, star-shaped flowers that attract bees. 'Brilliant' is a top cultivar and 'Carmen' has darker flowers. S. 'Herbstfreude,' or 'Autumn Joy' as it used to be known, grows up to 2 feet tall. It'll grow in most average soils in sun or some shade. Cut the dead flower stems off in winter or early spring. Zones 4–9.

Cranesbill

Geranium H. 10 inches, S. 3 feet
Long-lived and reliable, these deciduous perennials will grow in almost any soil in sun or shade. They make excellent weed-beating ground cover and they have wonderful flowers in a whole range of blues, whites, pinks and purples. Cut them back by about a third with shears, after flowering, to get another flush. 'Johnson's Blue' wins the prize but the list is endless. 'Ann Folkard' will spread up to 3 feet or more. Zones 4–9.

Euphorbia

Euphorbia H. 1–4 feet, S. 1–4 feet
A large group of unusual and deeply elegant plants with curious flowers made up of modified leaves. Most want a well-drained soil in full sun. *E. characias* subspecies *wulfenii* grows to 4 feet and is outstanding with grey-green leaves and yellowy-green "flowers." Cut out the flowered stems. *E. cyparissias* is low and spreading and *E. myrsinites* has pointy leaves. *E. griffithii* 'Fireglow' is red and, along with *E. schillingii,* likes a bit of shade. The milky sap is poisonous and can irritate the skin, but don't let that put you off. Zones 6–10.

Siberian iris

Iris sibirica H. 1 foot 8 inches–6 feet, S. 1 foot 6 inches
There are hundreds of irises to choose from; little dwarf, bulbous ones to great big, bearded, rhizomatous cultivars. The Siberian ones are among the easiest to grow and there are plenty of cultivars. They have narrow, grassy leaves and in early summer the stems have up to five flowers each. The colors of some are purple-blue with a splash of white; others are combinations of white, blue and yellow. They like a well-drained soil in sun or light shade. Zones 3–10.

Other dependable perennials
Coneflower, male fern, Japanese anemone, catmint

ballistic

Perhaps you're an impatient sort or maybe you'll be moving on in a few years. Both are good excuses for not bothering to plant the garden – but think again. Choose a few of these speed merchants and within only a year or two you will have turned a bare patch of dirt into a leafy paradise. There are trees and climbers for screening, shrubs for the main structural planting and perennials for splashes of color. Mix in a few of the annual plants described in *Grow Your Own*, chuck a bit of fertilizer about for an extra boost and you've got an instant garden. Keep an eye on them, though, because things can get a little out of hand; and if you stick around for a while you'll need to put pruning shears on your Christmas list.

Mallow

Lavatera 'Rosea' *H. 6 feet, S. 6 feet*
This really knows how to grow. It's even relatively cheap so this has to be the best value-for-money plant you can buy. It's a subshrub (doesn't quite make it as a shrub) with grey-green leaves and then masses of pink flowers all summer. Almost any reasonable soil will do, as long as it's in sun and sheltered from harsh winds. Prune it back in early spring to a low framework of stems. 'Barnsley' has almost white flowers with deep pink eyes and is slightly less vigorous. Zones 7–10.

Coneflower

Rudbeckia 'Herbstsonne' *H. 6 feet, S. 3 feet*
It's not so much that it's very fast growing but it's also very tall so you get obvious results very quickly. The deeply cut green leaves form a clump lower down and the large daisylike yellow flowers are massed above. The stems are very upright and sometimes need staking. If you deadhead the flowers they keep going from midsummer to late autumn. A moist but well-drained soil in sun or a little shade is best. *R. laciniata* 'Golden Glow' grows very fast. Zones 3–9.

Catmint

Nepeta 'Six Hills Giant' *H. 3 feet, S. 2 feet*
This perennial will fill in gaps between plants or at the front of the border in its first season, if you plant it in spring. Any well-drained soil in sun or partial shade is good. It has masses of light grey-green, aromatic leaves and in summer lots of lavender-blue flowers. The plant attracts bees and cats which sometimes roll around on it. Trim back the stems with shears at the end of the season. Zones 4–8.

Passion flower

Passiflora caerulea H. 30 feet, S. 2 feet
This is a very fast-growing, sometimes evergreen climber which needs trellis or wire for support. Plant in full sun or a little bit of shade in a well-drained but moist soil. From summer to autumn it has purply-blue and white flowers that are fascinating and really exotic. The orange fruits are edible but pointless. You can trim it up in early spring or leave it alone. A hard winter will knock it back to the main stem but it'll shoot up again. Zones 6–9.

Clematis

Clematis H. 15 feet, S. 3 feet
These have to be the fastest-growing flowering climbers. There are two readily available speed freaks. The evergreen *C. armandii* has leathery, green leaves and scented, white flowers in early spring. It'll really start to put some pace on in its second year. The common *C. montana* can get massive, up to 46 feet, but you should keep on top of the pruning so the abundant flowers are visible. Other favorites are *C. tangutica, C. alpina* and the large-flowered Jackmanii group. The roots should be shaded by other plants or stones and the leaves should be in sun or a little shade. A fertile, well-drained soil is best. Zones 4–9.

Eucalyptus

Eucalyptus gunnii H. 30–80 feet, S. 20–50 feet
Don't be alarmed by the size: although it can grow as much as 10 feet a year, you can keep it trimmed. That's the penalty for speed. As far as evergreens go, this has to be the fastest; it will be a real tree within a few years and is brilliant for screening ugly views. The blue-green leaves are rounded when young and elliptical when mature. It prefers a fertile, moist soil in sun. If you get sick of the tree, you can chop it off at ground level and it'll form a bush of new shoots. Thin them to a strong one and start again. Don't plant it near a building. Zones 8–10.

Pittosporum

Pittosporum tenuifolium H. 12–30 feet, S. 6–15 feet
Almost ideal for any garden, this large shrub starts off growing very fast for an evergreen and then slows down in older age so pruning isn't usually necessary. It is loosely conical in shape, and the stems are almost black, setting off the glossy green leaves perfectly. There are other varieties with variegated and purple leaves but they are generally smaller and in less of a hurry. Sun or partial shade in a moist soil is best. Zones 9–10.

Bamboos

BAMBOOS H. 10–20 feet, S. indefinite
There are heaps of bamboos but one of the fastest growing is *Phyllostachys aureosulcata* 'Aureocaulis.' It can form clumps of yellow canes up to 20 feet tall in its first year. *Pleioblastus variegatus* has green-and-cream-striped leaves and only grows to 3 feet but spreads quite fast. A perennial grass that spreads rapidly and can be a bit overzealous is *Phalaris arundinacea* var. *picta* (pictured left). All will grow in most soils but prefer it a bit damp in sun or dappled shade. Only problem: they are hard to get rid of. Zones 6–10.

California lilac

Ceanothus H. 20 feet, S. 20 feet
One of the fastest growing is *C. thyrsiflorus,* an upright evergreen bush that can reach 20 feet or more, and is especially good against a sunny fence or wall. It has large panicles of blue flowers in spring. The variety *repens* forms a low mound about 3 feet high and at least twice as wide. 'A.T. Johnson' grows to about 7 feet and has blue flowers, once in spring and again in autumn. They all like well-drained soil in full sun. Lightly snip evergreens back after flowering; in early spring, prune deciduous plants back to a framework. Zones 7–10.

Japanese anemone

Anemone x hybrida H. 5 feet, S. indefinite
An outstanding plant for filling in an empty corner. This perennial spreads quickly and can get a bit invasive once established, but it's worth the risk. It forms a clump of leaves at the bottom with erect flower stems above. The many cultivars have showy flowers from late summer to midautumn and are combinations of white, pink and yellow. It prefers a moist fertile soil but doesn't like being too wet in the winter. Zones 4–8.

Other ballistic plants
Cranesbill, euphorbia, cosmos, Canary creeper, abelia

architectural

These are striking plants that will stand out from
the mêlée of routine plantings. Each one has a
strong outline and an interesting shape. Set them
against a foil of less dramatic plants so they act
as focal points, or use them to create an individual
scheme of their own; choose their positions
carefully and give each the space it deserves for
a truly stylish garden. Most of them, including
the bulbs and perennials, look even better in pots
and containers but that can mean extra watering,
so give it some thought.

New Zealand flax

Ornamental onion

Allium giganteum H. 6 feet, S. 8 inches
You don't have to know your onions to grow some of these bulbous plants. Plant the bulbs in a decent well-drained soil in full sun and you should have success. The straight green leaves at the base aren't much, but they die back before the flowers come in summer. Large 4-inch globes of pink flowers are produced on very tall stalks. 'Globemaster' has much darker flowers on shorter stems. *A. karataviense* is a dwarf at 8 inches but has stunning, grey-green leaves. Zones 6–10.

Heavenly bamboo

Nandina domestica H. 6 feet, S. 5 feet
An elegant evergreen shrub that looks good in a border or in a container. It has upright, bamboolike stems with large compound leaves with many leaflets. These are reddish-purple to start with, then green and then red again in winter when some leaves may drop off. In summer it has lots of small white flowers followed by small red fruits. It needs a sheltered spot in full sun and a well-drained but moist soil. Zones 6–9.

Bear's breeches

Acanthus spinosus H. 5 feet, S. 3 feet
Popular with the Romans for decorating vases and friezes, this is one of the earliest recorded garden perennials. Its popularity is well founded because it has striking foliage and flowers. The leaves are deeply cut and wavy edged, forming clumps of dark green foliage. From late spring to midsummer it sends up these really tall flower spikes of white flowers with purple bracts. The whole thing is quite spiky. Grow in good soils in sun or light shade. *A. mollis* is also very good. Zones 5–9.

New Zealand flax

Phormium tenax H. 12 feet, S. 6 feet
A fine evergreen plant for a specimen in a container or as a focal point in a border. The dusky, blue-green, strap-shaped leaves are upright and up to 10 feet long. Tall greeny yellow or pale red flower spikes shoot up in summer. 'Bronze Baby' is only 2 feet tall with bronze leaves and 'Dazzler' is slightly bigger with purple and red stripes. *P. cookianum* has more arching stems. 'Cream Delight' has green and cream stripes and 'Sundowner' is a luxurious bronze, pink and cream. Grow in full sun in a well-drained soil. Zones 9–10.

Mullein

Verbascum olympicum H.6 feet, S. 2 feet
A rosette of large, woolly, silver-grey leaves at the base gives rise to an enormous, branching spike of similar, smaller leaves and saucer-shaped yellow flowers. It normally flowers in its second or third year and then promptly dies, but if you leave the flowers on it will self-seed. *V. bombyciferum* can be longer-lived. *Salvia argentea* is very similar with white flowers on 3-foot spikes. Grow in a well-drained soil in full sun. *V. olympicum* prefers alkaline soil. Zones 5–9.

Cabbage palm

Cordyline australis H. 10–30 feet, S. 3–12 feet
It's not really a palm at all but more of an evergreen shrub or tree. The lower strap-shaped leaves die as the plant grows and the straight brown trunk gets taller. Mature trees will send out a flower spike of creamy-white flowers and often this will cause it to branch. 'Purpurea' has bronzy purple leaves and there is a variegated form. *C. indivisa* is very similar although often taller and more prone to branching. In cold areas tie the leaves up against themselves in winter. They like well-drained soil in sun or light shade. Zones 10–11.

Globe thistle

Echinops ritro H. 2 feet, S. 1 foot 6 inches
Exactly as it sounds, this one. It's a herbaceous perennial with spherical, blue flower heads, nearly 2 inches across, in late summer. The leaves are spiky, like a thistle. 'Veitch's Blue' will often flower twice and has particularly dark blue flowers. *E. bannaticus* has flowers ranging from powdery blue-grey to the bright blue of 'Taplow Blue.' Grow in a poor, well-drained soil in full sun or a little shade. They'll self-seed if you don't deadhead. Zones 3–9.

Pineapple flower

Eucomis bicolor H. 2 feet, S. 8 inches
These unusual bulbs produce large, light green, strap-shaped leaves and then in late summer send up a 6-inch-long flower head on a purple-speckled stem. Each individual flower is pale green with purple-edged petals. Short green leaves stick out of the top giving the whole thing the appearance of a pineapple. Well, from a distance, anyway. Plant the bulbs 6 inches deep in well-drained soil in full sun against a wall. A mulch in winter protects them from cold weather. Zones 8–10.

Papyrus

Cyperus papyrus H. 6 feet, S. 4 feet
OK, so it's not actually hardy anywhere in the country but it could be worth the risk. The tall, triangular stems have a fluffy globe of green threads, each with a tiny brown flower at the tip. The Egyptians made paper by slicing strips of the pulpy stem and laying them flat in a criss-cross pattern before drying. Use soil-based potting mix. Grow the plant in a pot and stand it in a pond or a tub of water in the sun. Bring it inside for winter. Maybe Zones 10–11.

Italian cypress

Cupressus sempervirens 'Stricta' H. 20 feet, S. 10 feet
Known as a pencil conifer because of its shape, this slim, green tree will make your garden look rather Mediterranean. Be careful how you use it; individuals or odd-numbered groupings are best. Buy mature plants for instant effect but you might have to stake them at first. Snip off any leaves that spoil the shape. They must have a well-drained soil in full sun and be out of harmful winds. Zones 8–10.

Other architectural plants
Tree ferns, Japanese banana, American aloe, euphorbia, Japanese aralia

shade

Shaded areas can be quite soul-destroying, especially if the ground is dry, hard and full of roots. Fork in lots of organic matter to retain moisture, remove roots and other obstacles and dig each planting hole a little bit bigger than normal. It can take ages, but it's worth it in the end to turn a dingy brown corner into something green and lush. You can try pruning trees and shrubs to let in more light but if that's not possible then use some of the plants here, which thrive in a range of conditions from dappled sunlight to complete shade. Dry soil will usually mean fewer flowers and berries, and weaker, often leggy growth. As a general rule, variegated plants don't survive as well as green-leaved ones.

Hydrangea

Hydrangea H. 3–10 feet, S. 6–10 feet
Most of these deciduous shrubs will grow in a moist, well-drained soil in partial shade or sun but some prefer to be away from the light. The large *H. sargentiana* does best in deep shade; its large flat heads of bluey purple flowers are surrounded by larger white ones. *H. villosa* also likes the shade and is fairly similar. *H. quercifolia* has leaves like an oak that turn a marvelous bronze in autumn and panicles of white flowers from mid-summer. In spring cut back below the flower heads to a strong bud. Zones 4–9.

Male fern

Dryopteris filix-mas H. 3 feet, S. 3 feet
This is one of the most reliable and easy to establish deciduous ferns. It will grow in most soils, even dry ones, but does need shade. It's ideal for brightening up a dingy corner. Ferns look particularly good among rhododendrons, azaleas and foxgloves. The female fern, *Athyrium filix-femina,* is similar with light green fronds and a shuttlecock shape, and will grow in most soils as long as they're not very dry. Zones 4–8.

Lilyturf

Liriope muscari H. 9 inches, S. 1 foot 6 inches
The arching grassy leaves of this little gem form dense clumps of evergreen foliage. In autumn it sends up purple stalks with spikes of lilac-mauve flowers. It looks really good planted in large drifts under trees and shrubs in full or partial shade. A light, fairly fertile, well-drained soil is best and it prefers acid but it's not essential. 'Monroe White' has white flowers but must have full shade. 'John Burch' has gold variegated leaves and large flowers. Zones 5–10.

Christmas rose

Helleborus niger H. 1 foot, S. 1 foot 6 inches
This is one for the winter, when it is one of the few perennials to have leaves and flowers. It must be grown in light shade, preferably in a heavy neutral or alkaline soil where it will produce white, pink-flushed flowers from before Christmas until spring. *H. orientalis* puts up with a wider range of soils and has often greenish flowers. *H. x hybridus* is also more tolerant and its cultivars have beautiful flowers including green, purple, pink and yellow. Zones 4–9.

Foxglove

Digitalis purpurea H. 6 feet, S. 2 feet
These biennials look terrific in borders among other plants and will grow in almost any soil, shade or sun, except very dry or very wet. They don't need staking, they attract bees and they self-seed freely. The large, purple flowers appear on the stalks in early summer. 'Excelsior Hybrids' are a mixture of whites, yellows, pinks and purples. Other species include the yellow-flowered *D. grandiflora* and *D. lutea.* The latter prefers alkaline soil. Don't try eating them – they're deadly. Zones 3–10.

Bowles' golden grass

Milium effusum 'Aureum' H. 2 feet, S. 1 foot
A golden yellow grass that is perfect for growing in shade under shrubs and trees. It's perennial but stays half evergreen during winter before sending out new, glowing leaves in spring. The delicate, grassy flowers appear from late spring to midsummer. It prefers a moist soil but has to be well-drained. It self-seeds a bit, but never prolifically. Collect seed from the dry flower heads and sow *in situ* or divide the clumps in spring. Zones 6–9.

Japanese laurel

Aucuba japonica H. 10 feet, S. 10 feet
This evergreen shrub is easy to grow because it thrives in any soil unless it's waterlogged. The green-leaved sort likes deepest shade but the variegated ones prefer only partial shade. In midspring it has very small but interesting purple flowers and in autumn the female plants have red berries. 'Crotonifolia' is one of the best variegated cultivars; it's female with yellow speckles. Pruning isn't really needed but if you want to make it smaller, cut it back hard in the spring. Zones 6–10.

Skimmia

Skimmia japonica H. 20 feet, S. 20 feet
This plant will put up with almost anything including shade, pollution and neglect but it does like a fairly decent soil that doesn't dry out. Grow it under other shrubs and trees or in pots and containers. It has glossy green leaves, and this hermaphrodite form has flowers in spring and red berries later in the year. 'Rubella' is a male form that has neat ruby flower buds through autumn and winter. The female form has berries but only if it's been pollinated by a nearby male. It doesn't need pruning. Zones 7–9.

Rhododendrons and Azaleas

RHODODENDRON Various sizes
A mixed bunch of shrubs and small trees. Most have glossy evergreen leaves, which apart from the deciduous azaleas, have bronze autumn colors. All like a moist, well-drained compost-rich soil in some shade. The trumpet-shaped flowers can be yellow, white, blue, pink, red and orange and the plants are anything from a few inches to many feet high. The choice is endless. They do like acid soil so if you don't have it, try growing them in pots. Zones 4–10.

Cranesbill

Geranium macrorrhizum H. 1 foot 8 inches, S. 2 feet
I've also listed cranesbill under *Dependable Perennials* but they have to get another mention because most will grow in shade. This particular one not only thrives in shade but is brilliant for smothering weeds. It's almost evergreen with highly aromatic green leaves that turn red and bronze in autumn. In early summer it has clusters of pink or white flowers that aren't outstanding by geranium standards, but they're not bad. 'Ingwersen's Variety' is one of the best. Zones 4–8.

Other shade plants
Sweet box, Japanese anemone, Japanese aralia, toad lily, plantain lily

sun

If you've got hot, dry earth then count yourself
lucky: things could be much worse. Many things
will wither and die but choose carefully and you
can grow some wonderful plants. As a general
rule, herbs and silver-grey-leaved plants do well
in full sun with little water because they're adapted
to these conditions, as are plants with thick, fleshy
leaves. Once you've got plants established to cover
all the soil, they'll trap moisture and the range of
plants that you can grow will be increased. Working
compost into the soil and using a mulch will also
help. All the plants listed here will give a whole
range of colors, flower shapes and heights, so you
can mix them all up together for a lovely spread.

Sun rose

Cistus H. 3 feet, S. 5 feet
Ideal for poor, dry sunny soils with a little shelter from wind, these evergreen shrubs have saucer-shaped flowers in late spring and summer. They range from white to pink with yellow centers and some have blotches on the petals. *C.* x *corbariensis* has pink buds that open into white flowers with yellow centers. It forms a mound of attractive leaves 3 feet high and 5 feet wide. 'Silver Pink' is slightly smaller with dark green leaves and pink flowers. Prune only very lightly. Zones 8–10.

Sea holly

Eryngium alpinum H. 2 feet 6 inches, S. 2 feet
An absolute star. From midsummer to early autumn these amazing herbaceous perennials send up branching stems with thistlelike flower heads of an incredible shimmering blue. *E. giganteum* is slightly bigger with steel blue flowers surrounded by spiky, silver bracts, but it lives for only a few years. *E. planum* has light blue flowers and forms a clump of green leaves. All prefer a dry, not too fertile, well-drained soil in full sun. The flowers, which attract wildlife, are good for cutting and drying. Zones 3–9.

Tickseed

Coreopsis verticillata H. 2 feet 8 inches, S. 1 foot 6 inches
A mass of small, glowing, yellow flowers are produced by this perennial in summer. The feathery green foliage contrasts well with neighboring plants. 'Zagreb' is drought resistant but, unfortunately, they all spread quite slowly. Cultivars of *C. auriculata* and *C. grandiflora* are also very good. Grow them in a fertile soil in full sun or very light shade. Deadheading keeps the flowers coming. Bees can't keep away. Grow new plants from seed or divide clumps. Zones 4–9.

Cosmos

Cosmos bipinnatus H. 5 feet, S. 1 foot 6 inches
Possibly the best annual plant. Sow seed *in situ* in late spring. The feathery foliage quickly grows up and all summer you have a continuous mass of bold, saucer-shaped flowers of white, pink and crimson. Deadheading prolongs flowering but leave a few to self-seed. *C. atrosanguineus* is a lower-growing perennial with velvety, maroon flowers that smell like chocolate. It might need a bit of mulch to keep it warm in winter. Zones 7–10.

African blue lily

Agapanthus africanus H. 3 feet, S. 1 foot 6 inches
Huge round heads of trumpet-shaped blue flowers appear on stalks above clumps of lush green leaves from mid- to late summer. They are at home in the border but make elegant container plants. Moist, well-drained soil in full sun is best for them. There are plenty of cultivars, many of which are even hardier and more dramatic. 'Snowy Owl' has white flowers 4 feet high and 'Blue Giant' is equally big. 'Lilliput' is obviously quite small; only 15 inches high. Zones 7–10.

Hibiscus

Hibiscus syriacus 'Rose of Sharon' *H. 10 feet, S. 6 feet*
This upright shrub is the last to come into leaf and the first to lose them again in autumn so it needs to be slotted in between a couple of evergreen shrubs. Its saving grace is its flowering: masses of large, exotic, trumpet-shaped blooms from late summer to midautumn. 'Blue Bird' has bright, powdery blue flowers with a small red center, 'Diana' has 5-inch white flowers, 'Red Heart' is white with a red center. Pruning isn't essential but you can thin them out a bit in spring. They prefer a slightly alkaline soil. Zones 6–11.

Cobweb houseleek

Sempervivum arachnoideum H. 3 inches, S. 1 foot
An interesting succulent perennial that forms a low mat of rosettes that look as if they're covered in cobwebs. The small leaves that make up the rosettes vary from green to red. It sends up a rather phallic stalk with reddish pink flowers. *S. giuseppii* has leaves of a much lighter green tinged with red. All need full sun in a well-drained soil so you'll need to mix in some sand. They're excellent in pots and actually like poor soil. Zones 5–10.

Chinese plumbago

Ceratostigma willmottianum H. 3 feet, S. 5 feet
One of the best plants to come out of China, this twiggy deciduous shrub will grow in any well-drained soil in sun. The midgreen leaves have purple edges and turn red in autumn; the blue flowers last from late summer to autumn. Trim it back with shears in midspring to keep it in top condition. *C. plumbaginoides* is much lower growing and technically a perennial. The stems are red and the flowers a much brighter blue. Zones 6–10.

Sneezeweed

Helenium H. 5 feet, S. 2 feet
The daisylike flowers of this perennial come in a range of sumptuous reds, oranges and yellows that surpass most of their rivals. In summer and autumn it produces masses of flowers that keep coming for ages especially if you deadhead. Give them a good, moist, well-drained soil in lots of sun and they'll repay you handsomely. Taller cultivars may need a bit of staking. 'Bruno' has flower parts ranging from a dark crimson to a browny red. 'Septemberfuchs' is all oranges, browns and yellows. A bad choice for people with allergies. Zones 4–8.

Fountain grass

Pennisetum alopecuroides H. 2–5 feet, S. 2–4 feet
This perennial evergreen grass makes a clump of long, thin green leaves. In summer and autumn it has a profusion of fluffy flower heads, varying from greeny yellow to a sort of purple. In fact they look a bit like small squirrels' tails, but in a nice way. It likes a light, well-drained soil in full sun. In very cold areas give it a mulch in winter. Cut down all the leaves in early spring to encourage fresh, new growth. Zones 6–10.

Other sun lovers
Coneflower, lavender, catmint, globe thistle, star jasmine

moist

Some soils will remain moist whatever the weather.
The plants listed here will thrive in permanently
damp soils but can also suffer occasional dry
periods especially if they're in a little shade, so
there's no need to dash for the hose if a heat wave
comes along. Generally these all look pretty good
next to a pond or water feature of some sort
because that is how they've evolved – but
remember, they like it moist rather than boggy.
A minor drawback is that slugs and snails share
their passion for having wet feet, so keep an eye
out and thwart the blighters before they munch
their way through your leaves. A good mulch
will keep a lot of moisture in the soil and allow
you to grow these plants in borderline conditions.

Plantain lily

Hosta H. 6 inches–3 feet, S. 1–4 feet
A "must have" plant. Grown primarily for their clumps of bold leaves which are green, grey-blue, yellow or variegated. In summer they have tubular, sometimes scented flowers on stalks above the leaves. They need a moist soil that doesn't dry out and full or light shade. The yellow ones need a bit more light than most. *H. fortunei* var *'Aureomarginata'* has green leaves with a yellow edge, 'Halcyon' is blue-grey, 'Golden Prayers' is small and yellow and 'Honeybells' is green. *H. plantaginea* is highly scented. Zones 3–8.

Astilbe

Astilbe H. 3 feet, S. 2 feet 6 inches
The clumps of attractive, deeply-cut leaves range from light green to bronze in color. The flowers are feathery plumes in white, pink, crimson and red and they look really good next to a pond. In moist or boggy sites they can be grown in full sun but in drier soil they must have some shade. Fertile soils are best. Divide them every four years or so to keep them vigorous. 'Fanal' has dark green leaves and crimson flowers in early summer, 'Rheinland' is pink and 'Weisse Gloria' is white. Zones 4–9.

Primrose

Primula H. 4 inches–3 feet, S. 4 inches–1 foot 6 inches
Many, but by no means all, primroses like a deep, rich, moist soil. These herbaceous perennials grow from a rosette of green leaves and have a range of flower colors and formations. In summer, *P. vialii* (pictured here) sends up a 6-inch flower spike with crimson buds opening to a mauvy pink. *P. pulverulenta* is known as a candelabra primrose with distinctive tiers of deep red flowers on 3 foot stems in late spring and summer. *P. denticulata* has a ball of pink, mauve or white flowers about 18 inches tall. There are hundreds more species and cultivars. Zones 3–8.

Globeflower

Trollius chinensis H. 3 feet, S. 1 foot 6 inches
This moisture-loving perennial produces orangey yellow, buttercup-like flowers in midsummer. Cut the stems back hard after the first flowering, give a liquid feed and you'll get more flowers. Plant in sun or shade in a fertile soil that doesn't dry out. *T. x cultorum* 'Alabaster' has pale yellow flowers in spring and 'Orange Princess' has globular orange flowers a little later. Cultivars of *T. europaeus* are also very good. Zones 5–8.

Chinese rhubarb

Rheum palmatum 'Atrosanguineum' *H. 6 feet, S. 6 feet*
A stylish plant for people without enough space for gunnera (see *Leaves*). Grown for its large leaves and tall flower spikes, this plant grows best in deep, fertile, moist soils in sun or light shade. The young leaves are crimson, fading to green on the upper surfaces, and the flowers are a rich pink. 'Bowles' Crimson' is a good variety and 'Ace of Hearts' has smaller, heart-shaped leaves that have red veins and are deep purple underneath. Zones 5–9.

Ligularia

Ligularia dentata 'Othello' *H. 5 feet, S. 3 feet*
The kidney-shaped leaves are a rich purply green on top and a magnificent purple beneath. The flowers appear from midsummer to autumn and are a glowing, orangey yellow, borne on stalks that tower over the clumps of foliage. 'Desdemona' is very similar. *L. stenocephala* 'The Rocket' has toothed green leaves and lots of yellow flowers on tall, black stems up to 5 feet. They like a fairly decent, moist soil in full sun with a bit of midday shade. Zones 4–8.

Monkshood

Aconitum napellus
The erect stalks have dark green leaves and then in mid- to late summer lots of indigo blue hoodlike flowers towards the tops of the stems. They may need staking to stop them from flopping about. They'll grow in most soils in sun or some shade but do prefer things a little moist. Other shorter but excellent cultivars include 'Bressingham Spire' with deep violet flowers into early autumn and 'Ivorine' with white flowers from late spring. The foliage may irritate sensitive skin. Zones 3–8.

Inula

Inula hookeri H. 2 feet 6 inches, S. 2 feet
The finely cut, yellow, daisylike flowers appear from late summer to autumn above the clump of hairy, green leaves. These perennials like a moist soil in partial shade. *I. magnifica* will grow in waterlogged but sunny soils and produces large 6-inch flowers on stems up to 5 feet. *I. royleana* is much shorter at less than 2 feet and has orange flowers. It also prefers the sun as long as the soil doesn't dry out. Zones 4–9.

Meadow rue

Thalictrum aquilegiifolium H. 3 feet, S. 1 foot 6 inches
In summer, clusters of fluffy pink flowers open from tiny buds on erect stems. The foliage is equally important though, consisting of a large clump of delicate, pale green leaves. They like a moist soil in partial shade and look good beneath trees. 'Thundercloud' has dark purple flowers and 'White Cloud' has yellow-tinged white flowers. *T. delavayi* is later-flowering and taller, and its cultivar 'Album' has totally white flowers. Zones 5–9.

Sweet box

Sarcococca humilis H. 1 foot 6 inches, S. 3 feet
The glossy green leaves alone make this a worthwhile evergreen shrub. Couple that with the tiny, fragrant, white flowers and you're on to a winner – the winter flowers are then followed by small, round, dark blue fruits. It thrives in full or partial shade but does need a half-decent, moist soil out of harmful, cold winds. *S. confusa* is much larger, about 6 feet high and *S. hookeriana* var. *digyna* 'Purple Stem' has purply shoots and pink-tinged flowers. Zones 6–10.

Other plants that like it moist
Gunnera, Kaffir lily, loosestrife, papyrus, toad lily

scented

Plants with aromatic leaves often smell best on hot sunny days, otherwise the leaves will need to be touched or lightly bruised for the full effect. Choose their positions carefully so they're in sun or can be reached out to and touched. Camomile and thyme can be used as lawns and exude their scent when trodden on (see *Lawns*). Most of the flowers here are good for cutting and putting indoors. Plant them where they'll be appreciated: an evening-scented honeysuckle by an open window, fragrant clematis surrounding a seating area and aromatic herbs in pots around the patio or on the windowsill. For a good list of scented roses, I suggest contacting a specialist nursery.

Lemon verbena

Aloysia triphylla H. 10 feet, S. 10 feet
This is a deciduous shrub from Chile. The pointy leaves smell incredibly strongly of lemon and you can dry them for potpourris or herbal teas. It's not very hardy so you have to grow it against a sunny wall and mulch it in winter. It actually likes poor, dry soils. In early spring chop it back to a low framework of woody stems or train it against a wall and trim it lightly after flowering. The tiny white flowers appear in summer. Zones 8–11.

Jasmine

Jasminum officinale H. 40 feet, S. 2 feet
A fairly rampant, usually deciduous climber good for pergolas and trellises. It has quite attractive foliage but the white flowers from summer to autumn smell fantastic so it's good near a seating area. 'Affine' has pink-tinged flowers, *J. polyanthum* (pictured) is evergreen but not very hardy and *J. nudiflorum* has rather gaudy yellow flowers in winter. Thin out overcrowded growth after flowering. Grow in a fertile soil in sun or partial shade. Zones 6–11.

Curry plant

Helichrysum italicum subspecies *serotinum H. 1 foot 4 inches, S. 2 feet 6 inches*
This is an evergreen shrub with upright, woolly stems and silvery grey leaves. From summer to autumn, tight, flat flower heads of dark yellow are produced on the stem tips. Run your hands up the stems and you'll discover the powerful scent which gives this plant its name. Grow it in a fairly poor but well-drained soil. It will tolerate drought. Clip off the dead flowers with shears in spring. Zones 7–11.

Daphne

Daphne H. 2–6 feet, S. 2–5 feet
These shrubs all have sweet-scented flowers, but the drawback is that most are slow-growing and all are highly toxic. If that doesn't bother you, then choose from one of these. *D. alpina* is deciduous and grows to 2 feet with small, scented white flowers in late spring and early summer, *D. x burkwoodii* and its hybrids are much larger, up to 5 feet, and it has pink and purplish flowers, and *D. odora* is a good-looking evergreen with pinky white flowers from late winter. Grow in sun or light shade in a soil that isn't dry. Pruning unnecessary. Zones 4–10.

Lavender

Lavandula angustifolia 'Hidcote' *H. 3 feet, S. 4 feet*
Perfect for pots, edging paths and at the front of borders. The fragrant blue-purple flowers are produced from midsummer to autumn. Bees can't keep away. It's quite a compact shrub with thin, silvery grey leaves. It'll grow happily in most well-drained soils but sun is essential or it goes leggy. In spring, cut the flower heads and some of the foliage off with shears. 'Munstead' is a smaller cultivar and 'Loddon Pink' is also compact but with light pink flowers. Zones 5–10.

Clematis

Clematis rehderiana H. 22 feet, S. 10 feet
This is probably the best-scented clematis. The hanging, bell-shaped flowers are produced from midsummer right through to midautumn. They are ¾ inch long, small, yellow and in clusters. The leaves clothe a wall or trellis in purest green. They are vigorous and so put on a lot of growth each year. For pruning see group 3 under *Maintenance*. The roots should be shaded and the rest in sun. *C. recta* is a clumpy species but also sweetly scented. Zones 3–9.

Magnolia

Magnolia x soulangeana H. 20 feet, S. 20 feet
These beautiful, small, spreading trees come into flower and leaf at about the same time as the weather cheers up in midspring and you start to venture into the garden. The branches form an open framework that shouldn't need pruning unless the tree's too big for the space available. Some varieties are more strongly scented than others and the large, showy flowers range from white to burgundy. They like some shade. *M. grandiflora* 'Exmouth' has large, leathery, glossy, evergreen leaves and huge, fragrant, cup-shaped, creamy white flowers from late summer to autumn. Zones 3–9.

Honeysuckle

Lonicera H. 22 feet, S. 15 feet
A group of mainly deciduous climbers that have wonderfully scented flowers. Grow them up trees, over sheds or onto fences. *L. periclymenum* 'Belgica' has purple-red and yellow flowers in May and June, 'Serotina' flowers later from July to October. *L. japonica* 'Halliana' is sort of evergreen and has pure white flowers fading to yellow. Trim back after flowering but watch out for bird's nests. All like a moist, well-drained soil in sun or partial shade. Zones 4–9.

Regal lily

Lilium regale H. 2–6 feet
This lily wins the prize for being easy to grow and having attractive, very fragrant flowers. It's like the lilies you buy in flower shops. Tall stems with lots of small, shiny green leaves and then up to 20 or more white, trumpet-shaped flowers in midsummer. They have yellow centers and a purple flush on the outside. Plant the bulbs in autumn in a well-drained, not too alkaline soil in full sun. Stake as necessary. Zones 2–8.

Viburnum

Viburnum x bodnantense H. 10 feet, S. 6 feet
The rich red and light pink flowers of this deciduous shrub are perfect for cutting. This way you can appreciate their strong fragrance without having to go into the garden in late autumn to spring when they are in flower. It's an upright shrub with bronze leaves that turn green. Prune it lightly after flowering in spring to keep it under control. 'Dawn' is probably the best. Most soils will do, in sun or light shade. Zones 2–9.

Other scented plants
Plantain lily (*Hosta plantaginea*),
climbing roses (*Rosa* 'Golden Showers'), sweet box

curious

There are plenty of strange things going on in the plant kingdom, and we can grow a few odd things in our own gardens. Some of them are exotic with unusual, bizarre flowers; others are hallucinogenic or flammable or useful – providing drugs, alcohol and bath accessories. With a bit of patience, all can be quite easily grown. If you want to explore further there are some fantastic plants like bright blue corn on the cob, but I've been forced to leave them out because they might be hard to get hold of.

Bottlebrush

Callistemon subulatus H. 5 feet, S. 6 feet
The flowers of this Australian shrub are exactly like a bottle brush – well, almost. The pointy bright green leaves are exotic enough but the tiny red flowers in late summer, with long, fluffy stamens, are what make it special: packed together they make 2-inch-long brushes. *C. pityoides* is a smaller, more compact shrub with yellow flowers. Other species have much larger flowers but aren't reliably hardy. Grow in a moist, well-drained soil in full sun. Pruning can be done after flowering but isn't essential. Zones 8–11.

Angels' trumpets

Brugmansia syn. *Datura H. 6–12 feet, S. 5–8 feet*
The huge, dangling, trumpet flowers of this shrub are what make it special for gardeners; others like its narcotic properties – although the hallucinations don't start until just before the coma. All parts of this plant are poisonous. *B. x candida* has white or light yellow, night-scented flowers up to 11 inches long; 'Grand Marnier' and 'Knightii' are also excellent. In warm areas risk it outside; otherwise grow it in a pot in full sun and bring it indoors in winter. It likes moist, well-drained soil or compost, and you need to prune it almost to the ground in early spring. Zones 10–11.

American aloe

Agave americana H. 6 feet, S. 10 feet
Tequila is derived from the distilled sap of this Mexican desert succulent. The thick, fleshy green leaves have large spines along the edges and one particularly vicious one at the end. The leaves form a rosette and in summer mature plants send up a flower spike many feet high with clusters of yellow flowers. 'Marginata' is the best with thick, yellow leaf edges. It's hardy only in the mildest areas, so grow it in a pot and protect it in winter. It likes full sun in a very well-drained gritty or sandy soil. Zones 10–11.

Burning bush

Dictamnus albus H. 3 feet, S. 2 feet
The flowers and fruits of this clump-forming perennial produce an aromatic oil that you can set fire to in hot weather with no adverse affect to the plant. Try doing it on a warm summer's evening after dark for full effect. The leaves are lemon scented and the flowers, which appear in summer, are white or pink. Grow it in a dry soil in full sun or some shade. Avoid skin contact with the leaves. Zones 3–8.

Naked ladies (Meadow Saffron)

Colchicum autumnale H. 4–6 inches, S. 6 inches (leaves much bigger)
This huge, crocuslike flower is quite spectacular in the autumn when it sends up large purple flowers in clumps. The big leaves appear later and it needs to be grown among deciduous shrubs for full effect, preferably in a well-drained soil in some sun. Alternatively, you can stand a bulb on a shelf or windowsill and it will send out the large flowers without any assistance. When they fade, plant it outside in the ground. 'Alboplenum' has double white flowers and 'The Giant' has 3-inch, goblet-shaped blooms. Zones 4–9.

Quaking grass

Briza media H. 3 feet, S. 1 foot

This is an attractive perennial grass with delicate flower heads that dangle on the ends of thin stems, and in the slightest breeze the whole lot jiggles around in a trembling sort of way. It's all quite spooky. The flowers appear from late spring to midsummer and dry from green to a yellowy color. Grow it from seed or divide clumps and plant in any soil in sun or some shade. Zones 4–10.

Loofah

Luffa cylindrica H. 10 feet, S. 2 feet

You can use these curious gourds for cleaning your skin but you can also eat them. Grow it like a cucumber from seed: start it off on the windowsill in spring and then plant outside and grow against a trellis, although they actually do much better in a greenhouse. When the fruits are 6 inches long you can cook them like a marrow. Leave the fruits on the plant to mature into a skin brush. Zones 6–9.

St John's wort

Hypericum H. 2–6 feet, S. 2–6 feet

A bright red liquid oozes like blood from the crushed flowers of this perennial and is used as an antidepressant. Marketed as the "sunshine herb," *H. perforatum* is the natural Prozac – but don't try eating it, because it's harmful. Star-shaped bright yellow flowers appear all summer and it's ideal for a wild area. *H. calycinum* makes a very good, spreading ground cover in the shade, growing to about 2 feet tall and must be cut to the ground in spring. *H. hidcote* is an almost evergreen bush, growing to about 4 feet and it prefers a bit more sun. Moist, well-drained soils are best. Zones 6–11.

Chinese lantern

Physalis alkekengi H. 2 feet, S. 3 feet

This vigorous perennial has small, bell-shaped cream flowers in midsummer that give way to bright orange berries inside a red, papery pouch. As this ages, the pouch dries and turns into a skeletal framework of veins and the berry remains intact through the winter. If you want, you can cut them when they are young and dry them yourself. Plant in any well-drained soil in sun or some shade. Can be invasive. Don't eat them; they're a bit poisonous. Zones 5–8.

Toad lily

Tricyrtis formosana H. 2 feet 8 inches, S. 1 foot 6 inches

The star-shaped flowers of this perennial are really exotic in an orchid sort of way. In fact they're fully hardy and like a moist, well-drained soil in full or partial shade. Forking well-rotted organic matter into the soil before planting is advisable and a winter mulch is a good idea in very cold areas. The flowers are produced in autumn and are white or pink with purple spots and red stigmas in the center. Zones 4–9.

climbers

Some of these plants don't have a "spread"
because by their very nature they will grow up
rather than sideways, although if encouraged
they'll do both; pruning and training greatly alters
their ultimate size and shape. The good thing is that
whatever their size they hardly take up any space
on the ground and provide height and large blocks
of color. Some need the support of a trellis or
pergola, others are self-clinging and need only
to be pointed in the right direction before scaling
any wall. Some of the more woody climbers
need a good framework of sturdy horizontal wires
supported and held away from the wall by vine
eyes, available from hardware stores and garden
centers. Perennials and annuals can be grown in
the shelter of bushes and trees and others merely
need the protection of a wall.

Trailing abutilon

Abutilon megapotamicum H. 6 feet, S. 6 feet
This almost evergreen climber from Brazil should be grown in fairly good soil against a sunny wall or fence. The slender stems have small pointy green leaves but it's the curious red and yellow flowers that appear from summer through autumn that make it outstanding. Train it onto horizontal wires and trim it back lightly if it gets out of hand. There are loads of other excellent abutilons but they can suffer in cold areas. Zones 8–10.

Chilean glory flower

Eccremocarpus scaber H. 10–15 feet
Clusters of small, tubular, orangey flowers adorn this fast growing evergreen climber from late spring right through to the autumn. You need to grow it in full sun in a well-drained, fertile soil. Train it up wires or trellises and trim it back a bit in early spring to keep it under control. Other varieties produce yellow, pink and red flowers. It can get damaged in hard winters. Zones 10–11.

Ivy

Hedera H. 3 feet–indefinite
Ivy is a brilliant climber for covering walls and ugly sheds or as a backdrop for other plants. It's evergreen and self clinging, and you can prune it how you want, when you want. The green, white or yellow leaves come in all shapes, sizes and patterns: one of the best is 'Goldheart.' Ivy will live in most places; the green-leaved sorts tolerate shade and the variegated ones need a little shelter from cold winds. Zones 5–10.

Virginia creeper

Parthenocissus quinquefolia H. 30–50 feet
A deciduous climber ideal for pergolas and growing up into trees, the green leaves turn glorious shades of red in the autumn. Boston ivy, *P. tricuspidata*, has little suckers that help it cling to walls; it's a bit slow to start with and then it shoots up fast, and the autumn reds and purples are amazing. It looks particularly good on older houses, but don't let it grow into the roof tiles. Trim it back at any time. Sun or shade. Zones 3–9.

Ornamental vine (Crimson glory vine)

Vitis coignetiae H. 50 feet
You need a bit of space for this plant but it looks good on fences and pergolas. The large, heart-shaped leaves have a sort of brown felt underneath and they turn bright red in autumn before dropping off. The small grapes taste foul. Grow in well-drained soil in sun or partial shade. Trim the shoots back in winter and summer to keep it under control. The less vigorous *V. vinifera* 'Purpurea' has leaves in various shades of purple. Zones 4–10.

Flame creeper

Tropaeolum speciosum H. 10 feet
This perennial climber is happiest growing up through bushes and trees where it can produce masses of red flowers from summer to autumn. It prefers a moist, compost-rich soil in sun or partial shade but doesn't really like alkaline soils. It isn't fully hardy in colder areas but it's worth the risk. Pull down the dead growth in late autumn. The Canary creeper *T. peregrinum* is less fussy about soil and has yellow flowers (see self-seeders in *Grow Your Own*). Zones 8–10.

Chinese wisteria

Wisteria sinensis H. 28 feet
Lilac flowers like bunches of grapes cover a well-pruned plant in late spring before it comes into leaf. Good for pergolas and the sides of houses, it needs at least some sun but mustn't face east or the frosts will get the flowers. Sturdy wires are needed for support. Once established it grows damned fast, so you have to prune it to keep it in check (see *Maintenance*). If you can be bothered with the effort you'll be rewarded. Zones 6–9.

Star jasmine

Trachelospermum jasminoides H. 28 feet
A twining, evergreen climber best grown against a sunny wall and trained onto wires. The glossy evergreen leaves do turn slightly red in winter but it's the flowers that you're after. They appear through summer and are exactly like jasmine: the scent is fantastic. The variegated form is a less vigorous but, as far as I'm concerned, richer cousin. Trim it back lightly in early spring if you can be bothered. Zones 9–10.

Climbing roses

Rosa H. 10 feet, S. 6 feet
If you're a fan of roses, go for a scented climber. 'Golden Showers' is my favorite for a house wall: from summer to autumn it has loads of fragrant, clear yellow flowers 4 inches across. 'Climbing Iceberg' has a profusion of double white flowers. Train the main stems onto horizontal wires and in early spring prune flowered shoots by two-thirds. Ramblers are often less thorny but also less scented. Grow in a sunny, well-drained soil but don't replant roses in a previously used spot. Zones 2–9.

Cape figwort

Phygelius capensis H. 4 feet, S. 5 feet
Not 100 percent hardy, so this plant does need a warm wall or a bit of protection in winter if you live in a cold area. It has erect stems of dark evergreen leaves and in summer masses of slender, dangling, pale red flowers appear in loose clusters. *P. x rectus* 'Moonraker' has creamy yellow flowers and 'Winchester Fanfare' has red-pink ones. It likes full sun in a moist, well-drained soil. Grow it as a perennial and cut it down in spring, or as a lightly pruned shrub. Zones 7–9.

Other good climbers
Fig, lemon verbena, passion flower, honeysuckle, clematis

leaves

Ignore flowers for the moment and think about the
dramatic effects you can get from mixing foliage.
The Japanese actually prune the flowers off some
plants so they don't spoil the overall effect. Leaves
come in a whole range of colors: apart from a
multitude of greens there are yellows, reds, purples,
blues, greys and even black – and that doesn't
include the variegated ones made up of more than
one color. Add to that the variety of textures –
hairy leaves, delicate fronds and so on – and you
can get just about anything you can imagine in any
color, texture, size or shape. Emphasize contrasts
by planting a delicate fern next to the bold, glossy
leaves of a Japanese aralia or the dark, black leaf
blades of lilyturf.

Sedge

Japanese banana

Musa basjoo H. 15 feet, S. 12 feet
This classically-shaped banana palm is almost hardy. It will survive in warmer areas, although the huge 6- to 10-foot leaves may get torn by the wind. Plant it in full sun and in shelter next to buildings or among other plants, and fork in lots of compost. After cold winters the stems may need to be cut down but they will regrow. Mulching in winter will keep it warm. In summer it produces flowers and then horrible-tasting fruit. Zones 8–10.

Fountain bamboo

Fargesia nitida H. 15 feet, S. 5 feet
This graceful bamboo isn't too invasive like some of the others. It has dark, purplish canes which arch slightly at the top, where they produce many small, lance-shaped leaves. *F. murieliae* is a similar clump-forming bamboo with yellow stems. They are both good for screening along your fence lines or as specimens. They like a fertile soil but *F. nitida* won't tolerate full sun or wind. *Phyllostachys nigra* has black canes and grows well in pots. Zones 5–10.

Gunnera

Gunnera manicata H. 8 feet, S. 10–12 feet or more
This huge, stately perennial commands respect in any garden. It likes a constantly moist soil but can survive in drier soils if you water during drought; it just won't get very big. The rhubarblike leaves can get up to 6 feet long. You can grow this plant in a small garden but only if you give it the space it deserves. It likes sun or partial shade in a rich soil with shelter from the wind. In winter, cut the leaves off and lay them over the crown. Zones 7–10.

Japanese aralia

Fatsia japonica H. 5–12 feet, S. 5–12 feet
There's a place in most gardens for one of these classy evergreen shrubs. The large, shiny, lobed leaves are what make it outstanding. Grow it in a fertile, moist but well-drained soil in sun or shade but shelter it from harmful winds. In autumn it produces globes of tiny, creamy white flowers followed by round, black fruit. If it's in conditions that it likes, it will spread sideways quite quickly. No need to prune. Zones 8–10.

Wormwood

Artemisia 'Powis Castle' H. 2 feet, S. 3 feet
There are lots of species and cultivars of *Artemisia* and all are grown for their aromatic grey and silver leaves. This one is a perennial that grows like a shrub. It has fine, feathery, silver-grey leaves and although it does have yellow flowers in summer these are not important. Plant it in full sun in a well-drained soil, give it a winter mulch and cut it back in spring to keep it compact. Watch out for aphids on the young shoots. Zones 3–8.

| Sedge | *Carex hachijoensis* 'Evergold' *H. 1 foot, S. 1 foot 2 inches* |

This tufty sedge forms a mound of thin, green, grassy leaves with a central yellow stripe. It likes a moist soil in sun or partial shade. Plant it in groups with other grasses and sedges. It also looks pretty good in pots with a gravel mulch. *C. fortunei* 'Frosted Curls' is another evergreen perennial but with thinner, silver-green leaves that look almost dead but are somehow attractive. It doesn't like very wet or very dry conditions. Zones 3–9.

| Olive | *Olea europaea H. 30 feet, S. 30 feet* |

This slow-growing evergreen tree straight from the Mediterranean is best grown in a large container or in a sunny, sheltered spot. A deep, well-drained soil is best. The small, leathery, grey-green leaves and interesting branch structure make this a worthwhile risk. It is hardy only in frost-free areas. In summer it has tiny, fragrant white flowers and, if it's hot enough, olives. Zones 8–10.

| Black lilyturf | *Ophiopogon planiscapus* 'Nigrescens' *H. 8 inches, S. 1 foot* |

Possibly the blackest leaves in the plant kingdom. This evergreen perennial makes a little clump of arching, strap-shaped leaves. It has small purply white flowers in summer and then pea-sized black fruits. The ordinary green form is also attractive and *O. japonicus* has some variegated cultivars. Grow them in a moist, well-drained and preferably acid soil in sun or some shade. A carpet of them makes stunning ground cover. Zones 7–10.

| Tree fern | *Dicksonia antarctica H. 20 feet, S. 12 feet* |

Huge ferny fronds emerge from the top of a thick brown trunk, which is a mass of roots and old leaf bases. These giant ferns are best bought large because they're actually quite slow growing. Plant them in the ground in a moist soil in shade – you can even stand them in water. They withstand frost but may not be fully hardy. The large ones are ludicrously heavy so don't get any ideas about bringing them in for winter. Zones 9–10.

| Japanese cedar | *Cryptomeria japonica* 'Elegans' *H. 20–30 feet* |

An upright but irregularly-shaped evergreen conifer. It has feathery foliage that is bluish green when young and takes on a reddish bronze tinge in autumn and winter. It will grow in most soils although it prefers a moist, well-drained one in sun or some shade. Grow in a mixed border or as a focal point. Pruning isn't necessary but untidy plants can be rejuvenated by cutting to 2 feet 6 inches high in spring. 'Elegans Compacta' is the same thing only smaller. Zones 6–9.

Other leafy plants
American aloe, heavenly bamboo, Chusan palm, pittosporum, Japanese laurel

trees

The choice of trees is enormous and it's impossible
to cover them all here. What I've done is make
a selection in an attempt to offer something for
everyone. Remember not to plant them too close
to walls and buildings because the roots can
damage foundations and septic systems quite
severely. Think ahead: you probably want to block
an ugly view, provide shade or just put a bit of
height and color into the garden. What you choose
will be determined by how long you can wait and
what the ultimate size is. On the other hand, don't
be afraid to plant something for the future that
will be around long after you've become fertilizer
yourself. Just remember that the 6-foot baby tree
you plant now may grow into an 80-foot giant.

Contorted willow

Stag's horn sumach

Rhus typhina H. 15 feet, S. 20 feet
This small tree has velvety, rust-colored stems that give it its common name. The dark green leaves turn yellow, orange and red before dropping in autumn and strange conical fruits are produced at the tips of the branches in summer. 'Laciniata' has finely cut leaves. Grow them in any half-decent soil, but in full sun for the best autumn color. Pruning isn't essential but the suckers (sort of shooting roots) can make it invasive. Zones 2–10.

Black locust

Robinia pseudoacacia 'Frisia' *H. 80 feet, S. 50 feet*
It's fast growing and does turn into quite a big tree so make sure you put it away from the house and other trees. The fresh, golden yellow leaves in spring become greener as time goes on until they turn orangey yellow in autumn and drop off. The stems are quite thorny, so it's not much good for climbing and if you prune, do it in late summer so it doesn't bleed. Poor, dry soils will do, but it prefers a moist spot. Zones 5–10.

Sweetgum

Liquidambar styraciflua H. 80 feet, S. 40 feet
It's ultimately far too big for a small garden so one of the smaller cultivars is essential in a small space. This majestic tree has green, maple-like leaves that in autumn turn the most amazing shades of purple, orange and red especially if given full sun. It will grow in most soils. 'Golden Treasure' has variegated leaves and is slower growing and much smaller than the standard one. 'Moonbeam' has creamy-yellow leaves and good autumn color. Zones 7–9.

Contorted willow (Dragon-claw willow)

Salix babylonica 'Tortuosa' *H. 50 feet, S. 25 feet*
The strangely twisted shoots of this deciduous tree are what make it worthwhile, especially in winter. The green leaves are also twisted and there are greeny yellow catkins. It grows quite quickly into a neat shape but takes a while to get to full size. Most soils will do except for shallow chalk. Prune it in early spring if you need to keep it small. The twigs are good for a snazzy flower arrangement. Zones 2–9.

Crab apple

Malus H. 15–25 feet, S. 10–25 feet
Superb trees for small gardens, grown for their scented flowers and small, applelike, ornamental fruit. There are stacks to choose from and most have rounded heads on a single trunk. 'Katherine' has large, double, pale pink flowers in late spring that fade to white and are followed by tiny yellow and red fruits. 'Marshall Oyama' has pink flowers and larger fruits and 'Van Eseltine' has pink flowers and is more upright. They like a moist, well-drained soil. Zones 2–8.

Himalayan birch

Betula utilis var. *jacquemontii H. 60 feet, S. 30 feet*
Smaller and slower-growing than the common silver birch and with a much more open branch system, therefore casting less shade. The leaves are dark green and the bark is brilliant white. Cultivars to watch out for are 'Jermyns' and 'Silver Shadow.' If you have the space, an ordinary birch does a better screening job. Snipping the leading shoots keeps it small but serious pruning spoils the outline in winter. Moist soils are best but don't plant near buildings. Zones 2–9.

Snowy mespilus

Amelanchier lamarckii H. 30 feet, S. 40 feet
A small, deciduous tree that is a good all-rounder; the young bronze leaves turn green as they mature and the autumn colors of orange and red are marvelous. Lots of small, white flowers appear in midspring and these are followed by small, purply fruits. The birds love these trees. *A. canadensis* is incredibly similar but smaller and sometimes more of a bush. Sun or partial shade is fine in any moist, well-drained soil as long as it's not alkaline. Pruning isn't really necessary. Zones 3–9.

Strawberry tree

Arbutus unedo H. 25 feet, S. 25 feet
A spreading evergreen tree with glossy green leaves a bit like a bay leaf. The bark is reddish brown and flaking. The small white flowers give way to hanging, yellow and red strawberrylike fruits in the autumn. *A.* x *andrachnoides* is quite similar. They are fairly slow growing. Any fertile, well-drained soil, even alkaline, is fine but they don't like cold winds. They make good container plants and are one of the few interesting evergreen trees. Zones 7–9.

Paperbark maple

Acer griseum H. 30 feet, S. 30 feet
Of the hundreds of different maples, some are perfect for small gardens. This one is ultimately quite big but it grows so slowly that it will always be a small tree as far as you're concerned. The bark is orangey-brown and constantly flaking and the green leaves turn orange and scarlet in autumn. The Japanese maples are also very good: try any of the cultivars of *A. palmatum*. They like a decent, moist, well-drained soil in a bit of shade, and shelter from cold winds. Zones 3–9.

Chusan palm

Trachycarpus fortunei H. 70 feet, S. 8 feet
The hardiest of palms, but even so it won't like very cold areas. The large, fan-shaped evergreen leaves are carried at the top of a single, brown trunk. Small yellow flowers are often borne in summer. It makes an excellent specimen in well-drained soil or you can grow it in a large container. It prefers full sun out of cold winds; try it against buildings for protection. *Chamaerops humilis* is another good palm but slightly less hardy. Zones 9–10.

Other trees in this book
Magnolia, tree fern, eucalyptus, fig, cabbage palm

botanical pariahs

These are plants that I particularly loathe and, at the risk of seeming like a horticultural fascist, you really must give them a wide berth. Make the wrong choice of plant and you could regret it every time you look out the window. Garden centers have always stocked these pariahs out of habit, and people have always bought them because, however hideous, everyone else has got them and it's a safe bet. So what you'll find overleaf is a list of things not to buy, and reasons why you shouldn't. Your mother will be horrified – she probably swears by them, just like she swears by her old Chrysler LeBaron. The heights and spreads listed are ultimate to give you an idea of some of their horrifying proportions.

Dahlia

Leyland cypress

x Cupressocyparis leylandii H. 120 feet, S. 15 feet
If you live in a 1960s ranch in suburbia with a neighboring skyscraper this could be the plant for you. It might seem like a good idea at the time but the maintenance is phenomenal and it looks atrocious. Fast-growing evergreen ideal for screening – but you'll live to regret it. Nothing grows underneath, it needs constant trimming, leaves a rash on your skin and ultimately grows into an ugly monster. Zones 6–9.

Snowberry

Symphoricarpus albus H. 6 feet, S. 6 feet
A deciduous shrub with its roots firmly in the past. The white berries glisten on the bare winter stems like tasteless Christmas ornaments. Children enjoy throwing them at each other so they have some use, but for an added surprise, they are of course poisonous. Constantly sending out suckers, this tramp of a plant spreads around the garden and would happily take over the whole thing. Zones 3–7.

Japanese cherry

Prunus 'Amanogawa,' 'Kanzan' H. 25 feet, S. 12 feet
Many flowering cherries are beautiful trees like the one pictured, and often herald the onset of summer. However, these are two to avoid. 'Amanogawa' is a tall column of a tree which looks as if the branches have been bound against the trunk by a string of pink blobs, giving the impression of something trying to escape. 'Kanzan,' on the other hand, is an inverted pyramid on a stick, with brash, cerise-pink blooms. If you want a cherry, choose one with a shape more akin to the trees you drew as a child. Zones 3–9.

Greater periwinkle

Vinca major H. 1 foot 6 inches, S. indefinite
Is it a shrub? Is it a climber? This is truly a plant with an identity crisis. As ground cover it is too sprawling to suppress weeds and it winds itself into other plants, not having the guts to support itself. It is vigorous and impossible to contain or eradicate once established. The lesser periwinkle, *Vinca minor*, should be selected in preference every time. Purple-blue flowers are around for at least six months on the evergreen foliage, which is more compact. This is a ground-cover plant that knows it's a ground-cover plant. Zones 7–11.

Russian vine

Fallopia baldschuanica H. as tall as a house x S. several small villages
Its other name is Mile-a-minute, which gives an idea of the speed at which this climbing menace grows. Other books will exhort its potential for rapidly screening a shed or an unwelcome view. Only if the shed is an oil refinery and the view is Newark should you consider this. It will swamp your garden and explore your neighborhood. An expert burglar, it will force an entry through your roof and claim squatters' rights. Its sister, Japanese knotweed, can burrow under an expressway and spring up on the other side. Court them at your peril.

Rue

Ruta graveolens H. 3 feet, S. 2 feet 6 inches
Although it has many interesting medicinal properties, this shrub is now a common ornamental. Granted, it's an attractive blue-grey and it is sort of evergreen, which accounts for its popularity. But what's in a name? A lot. *Graveolens* is Greek for "strong smelling." I don't know what the Greek for "stinks like cat pee" is, but it would be far more appropriate. It retards the growth of sage, basil and figs and even slugs don't like it. If you like the color, choose an alternative, like sedum, euphorbia or wormwood. Zones 8–9.

Viburnum

Viburnum rhytidophyllum H. 15 feet, S. 12 feet
Apart from having a stupidly long botanical name, this evergreen shrub is suitable only for a very large garden with a bit at the back that no one ever sees. This garden center favorite of little merit is interesting because it looks as though it is permanently on the brink of death. Its large, corrugated leaves droop like it has given up and just doesn't care any more. Zones 3–9.

Hybrid tea roses

Rosa H. 6 feet, S. 2 feet
These are the roses with which everyone is familiar: think of a rose and this is the type that's conjured up. On the plus side they are sweetly scented and come in myriad colors. On the minus side they are a maintenance nightmare: constant deadheading, pruning twice a year and a charitable host to countless pests and diseases. A bit of wind and rain and the flowers are over, revealing their true colors: nothing but a few mottled leaves and some thorny sticks to savage you during pruning. Zones 6–7.

Pampas grass

Cortaderia selloana H. 10 feet, S. 5 feet
This ornamental grass does have a certain seventies chic – indeed it's very "Mike Leigh" – but it's also quite hideous. The long, silvery plumes arise from a clump of slender, arching leaves armed with thousands of fine teeth. Walking past one of these is like sharing a bed with a tiger shark, only worse. There are so many fabulous grasses available now that thankfully it has relinquished its crown to other, more worthy plants. Zones 7–10.

Cactus flowered dahlia

Dahlia H. 5 feet, S. 3 feet
Perhaps I hate these hideous, gaudy flowers because they were just about the only thing growing in my mother's garden when I was little – maybe it's a Freudian thing. Or maybe it's because they look so totally artificial, as if they were made cheaply somewhere in Asia. The huge flower heads form a pom-pom of curved, pointy petals. As if that isn't bad enough, they have the audacity to come in bizarre combinations of pink and white, yellow and peach and much worse. Zones 6–10.

getting planted

What you need

Spade, fork, boots, compost, fertilizers, pruning shears, garbage bags. (See also Tools on page 29.)

When you plant

It's OK to plant at almost any time of year unless the ground is rock hard through drought or frost. However, while this is useful for impulse buys, it's not the best approach for larger-scale plantings.

Early autumn is the absolute optimum time, when the soil is still warm, damp and workable. The roots can grow a little before winter and the new plant is established and ready for the whole of the next growing season.

Tender plants and some evergreens are better started in spring, which is the next best planting season. The soil is warming up, the ground is still moist and once the frosts are over the risk of damage to less hardy plants is eradicated.

Preparing your ground

Weeding

Weeds are complete horrors. They're invasive; they compete with your plants for space, light, water and nutrients; they grow up through your shrubs; and they smother and kill. Your aim must be to eradicate weeds and get rid of bare soil so they can't grow back. A good season to weed in is the spring. It means you can get on top of things early in the year and cut your work right down.

The most important thing is to weed things out before they flower so they don't spread even more seed everywhere.

If you're revamping a weedy area of the garden, then you have to dig the weeds out by hand, but if time isn't an issue you can do the organic thing and cover them with black plastic or even old carpet, although it's all a bit ugly. As I said in *Compost* it can all be covered in compost to make it look more pleasing. If you're planting a new bed then make sure it's weed-free first or you'll be forever fighting a losing battle. Organic suppliers sell propane or kerosene-fueled contraptions to burn weeds to death (see *Buyer's Guide*).

The good thing about thorough hand weeding is that the soil gets forked over and aerated as you go, relieving compaction, improving drainage and exposing soil-borne pests to predators. Lumpy clay soil is subsequently broken down by frosts so if you get the time and want to plan ahead a bit, do it in the autumn or winter. Areas of freshly dug soil do look good and will make your toils seem more worthwhile each time you look out the window. It won't be colonized by weeds over the winter and then you're just left with the relatively easy task of planting in the spring.

For more on weeds see *Maintenance*.

Digging and planting

Once you've dug over the bed for the first time, spread compost or manure (see *Compost*) and fork it in so that it's actually mixed with the soil.

You don't need to do this thoroughly. Work from a back corner to the front of the bed to avoid trampling on your handiwork. Large lumps can be broken up by banging them with the back of the fork tines. Dragging the tips over the soil helps to level it roughly but don't worry too much about this as once the plants are in, the final leveling comes naturally.

OK, so now the ground is prepared. If you left it during the winter you might need to remove a few weeds, break up some large lumps of soil (which should now be easy) and possibly rake off some unrotted leaves from last autumn.

Next go and buy your plants. Try not to get them before you need them (see *Buyer's Guide*) because being in pots, they'll dry out rapidly, blow over and get damaged.

Even if they've only just been bought or delivered, water them well before you start. A dry plant will struggle to get established.

Spread them out on top of the soil, according to your planting design, but remember not to space them evenly, which is the temptation. Take note of the planting distances or spread of the individual species. Sometimes this is on the label; if not, look them up. Getting it right now will eliminate drastic pruning, digging and transplanting in later years.

Plant ground cover and things that knit together fast so there isn't any bare soil. I can't tell you how important this is. While perennials are getting established, which will take at least three years,

sow annuals and things that self-seed to fill the gaps and compete with the weeds but not your other plants. Excellent weed-smothering ground cover includes *Geranium macrorrhizum* and St John's wort.

Remember the points in *Structure and Color*. Stand back, look at it, and imagine the garden in three or five years, the plants knitted together, the bare soil gone. Move things around, try things out. Hold your hands out in thin air to imagine heights and spreads and generally look silly in front of the neighbors. Visualize.

Start at one end and work in one direction and plant the ones at the back first.

Dig a hole roughly three times the volume of the pot and stack the soil in a couple of piles near the hole. Loosen the soil in the bottom with a fork to help drainage and make things easier for the roots. Throw in a pot full of compost, some fertilizer and a bit of the excavated soil. Mix it up with the spade. There should still be enough room to place the plant pot in the hole.

Take the pot in one hand, fingers flat and on either side of the stem at the base of the plant, and tip it upside down. With the other hand, remove the pot. This may require a gentle tap of the rim on a solid object or a light squeeze of the sides. If there are roots growing through the drainage holes cut or pull them off; they're useless anyway (see *Buyer's Guide*).

If the roots are pot bound – in other words if you can see mostly roots and not much soil – it is

worthwhile to gently tease some loose. Otherwise they may continue to grow round in circles, and stop the plant from growing.

Place the root ball in the hole. The top of it should be just below the level of the surrounding earth. Now backfill with soil, simultaneously holding leaves and stems out of the way. Three hands are useful but if you have only two, that will suffice.

Now tread the soil down with your heel, gently but firmly. Use the weight of your body and don't stamp (gardening is meant to be relaxing, after all). The idea is to remove air pockets from around the roots so they can function properly, and to anchor the plant so it doesn't flap about in the wind. The end result should be a shallow saucer-shaped depression made by your foot around the base of the plant. This will collect water, which will drain directly to the root zone while the plant becomes established.

However, if the top of the root ball is visible, you've got it wrong – the soil will settle, exposing the roots, which will desiccate and cause suffering and eventual death. One exception is the Rhododendrum family, which doesn't like to be planted too deeply. If the soil is too high around the base of the plant this may cause it to rot. Dig it up and start again. You'll soon get the hang of it.

You will notice that you've got some soil left over but don't worry because unless you're working in a tiny space you can always distribute it over the beds as you go. Don't be afraid to lift up the skirts of an overhanging bush and throw some under there. It will actually do it some good.

Watering and mulching

Now water the plants in, preferably with a hose and a gentle sprinkler nozzle, or a watering can. Do them individually, and see how the water collects in the "saucers" before sinking into the soil. You'll find out now if you got the planting depth correct. If you start to see roots appearing at this stage, you'd better not put the spade away yet.

To get the plants established you must water regularly, especially during warm or dry periods. A couple of pints per plant is a rough guide. You can use a sprinkler but much of the water will be wasted – not good if you pay for water or are worried about water conservation. Even if it rains (unless it's torrential), you'll still have to do it – imagine how much rain you'd need to put several pints onto a square yard of ground. In warm weather, water in the morning, before the full heat of the day. This helps plants to wake up (nothing like a cold shower to start the day), and the leaves will dry off by evening. If leaves stay wet overnight it invites fungus diseases. Get a little plastic rain gauge, and put about an inch of water on your garden every week. Water deeply – frequent sprinkles encourage shallow root growth, which is bad.

Mulching (see *Compost*) isn't essential but is a very good idea, especially with new plantings. It traps moisture and slows evaporation. It also keeps the heat in, which is extremely important, especially in autumn, for encouraging root growth and establishing the plant. Finally, it reduces weeding, a big plus.

Top tips:

— Don't try to plant too much at once. You'll get bored and go off the whole business.

— Don't get lazy. Keep those holes big. It really is good exercise and cheaper than joining a gym. Have you ever seen a fat gardener?

— Avoid planting in hot weather. You'll be out watering constantly and it's bad for the plants.

Special cases

Trees. Dig the hole as above only make it bigger. Pound a tree stake straight in so that the top protrudes about 2 feet above ground level and put the root ball into the hole so that the trunk is about 6 inches away from the stake. Fill the hole up and mix in moisture-retaining polymer granules (see *Containers* on page 164). Firm the tree in and fix a proper tree tie between trunk and stake. Water it in well and put down a mulch. Water regularly for the first year until the tree is established, and remember to slacken off the tree tie every year or so, so that it doesn't cut into the trunk and kill it.

Climbers. Plant these as for any other shrub, but don't plant right up against a wall because you'll restrict the root growth. Lean them towards the wall when you plant them. They are best trained on supporting trellises or wires fixed horizontally to walls or fences.

Bulbs and Corms. For extra color at ground level, plant bulbs in gaps among other plants. The usual time to plant them is in the autumn when they hit the shops in a big way but remember you can always buy them flowering in pots in the spring and then plant them in the garden when they're finished. There are hundreds to choose from but the old favorites – daffodils, crocuses, tulips and snowdrops – are the most reliable. As a rough guide, plant bulbs two to three times their own height deep. Dig a hole, chuck in a bit of fertilizer and plant them in irregular clumps, never in lines. After flowering, let the leaves die and go yellow before you pull them off. Try something a little more unusual like winter aconites, cyclamen or the autumn-flowering naked ladies (meadow saffron).

Transplanting. You may need to move an established plant to a different part of your garden. Most herbaceous perennials are easily moved in early spring and you can divide and revitalize them at the same time (see *Grow Your Own*). Shrubs are a bit more complicated because they have much larger root systems that inevitably get damaged during the move. Ideally you should start work the year before the move. Dig a trench around the plant and fill it with loose compost. This allows the plant to grow lots of important little roots and reduces the shock.

In reality, you're more likely to do it on impulse. To minimize the suffering, follow some basic rules: move plants in spring when the weather is warming up and plants are about to break dormancy; water them well before the move and avoid really sunny days; have the new hole prepared and take as much soil and fine roots with the plant as you can; replant immediately and water until established.

grow your own

Plants from a garden center aren't dirt cheap. It's fair enough if you just make the odd purchase to fill in a gap but if you're planning to revamp an entire bed or undertake a major overhaul of the garden, then costs can start to get a bit alarming. On top of that, even when you've finished planting, there's more bare soil than you can shake a stick at.

The simple and extremely satisfying solution is to propagate your own plants. Propagating, or making your own plants, can be as simple as flinging a handful of seeds onto a bed or digging something up and chopping it in half. Easier still, you can plant things that spread themselves around by seed and you don't have to do a thing. Marvelous.

Sowing the seed

Direct sowing

Sowing seed straight into the ground is staggeringly simple. It's how I first became interested in gardening as a child. I remember being amazed and even slightly confused by everything that came up when I didn't really do anything. It was like magic.

Sow seeds in drifts, to fill the gaps between existing shrubs and perennials – but wait until the frosts are over and the soil doesn't feel freezing cold if you crumble it between your fingers. The good thing about annual seeds is that you can try something new every year.

Fork over the ground, rake it level and remove weeds and large stones. Take a stick and scratch zigzag lines into the soil, sow your seed thinly into this and cover it over lightly with soil. As the seed germinates you'll be able to tell the difference between weeds and what you want to keep. When the seedlings are big enough to handle, thin them out to about an inch apart. Hold them by the lowest seed leaves, not the stem, and carefully replant them if you have room. Water seed and seedlings well.

Good seeds for springtime direct sowing (i.e., where you want the plants to grow) are: cornflower, clarkia, convolvulus, African daisy, nasturtium, Californian poppies, gypsophila, toadflax and sunflowers (the last are one of the best contenders). Marigolds, alyssum, candytuft, nigella and poppies can be sown in either spring or autumn.

The lazy way

Some seed can be scattered onto roughly weeded ground after very little preparation. Just have a look round a bird-table: it's amazing what grows from the seed that falls off. My grandmother had a fine crop of cannabis in her garden before she sent it off to Kew Gardens for identification. The shock of the reply nearly finished her off. Choose the right things like foxglove and maybe a wildflower mix and they'll set seed, and new plants will come up year after year. But don't expect a tremendous success rate with this method.

Nasturtium

Sunflower

Sea holly

Euphorbia

Sowing seed indoors

Sowing kit. You'll need: seed trays, seed starting mix, vermiculite, copper fungicide solution, a dibber (a specially shaped plastic stick), waterproof labels, waterproof marker pen, clear polyethylene or glass, and a sieve (for garden use only).

The whole point of indoor sowing is to get things started off much earlier than you could outside; also many seeds need a slightly higher temperature to wake them up and get them going. The simple way to do this is on your windowsill or some other indoor space in the warmth, but make sure you read the packet because some seeds actually need dark to germinate.

If you've got room, a seed tray is best. You can buy them really cheaply but small pots will do. You also need to buy a sterile seed starting mix – don't reuse old stuff. Put the mix into the tray and remove any lumps, and press it down evenly with the bottom of another tray or anything on hand that's flat. You can mix vermiculite (see page 163) in with it. This holds nutrients well and lets the new roots penetrate more easily. Water the mix with a copper fungicide solution to prevent fungus diseases and rot. If you do this later you'll wash the seeds all over the place. Don't forget to label everything and keep the packets so you know what to do with the seedlings later.

Pour the seed into a cupped hand and lightly tap it with the other as you distribute the seed evenly over the surface. Cover this with a thin layer of vermiculite or fine mix. Then cover the tray with a sheet of glass or some plastic food wrap and make a sort of mini-greenhouse. It shelters the seeds from damaging drafts, keeps the moisture in and retains heat.

As an alternative you can sow seeds directly in pots. This works for larger seeds and things like sweet peas that don't like having their roots disturbed when they go to their final place in the ground. Clear polyethylene bags can be fixed over the top with elastic bands for the greenhouse effect.

Care. Pop them on a windowsill but avoid direct sunlight, which can raise the temperature and cook the seedlings; too little light and they'll go all leggy. As they germinate turn the trays around occasionally to stop the seedlings leaning over towards the window. Remove the glass or plastic wrap every now and then because excess condensation can cause fungus trouble and cuts down light.

All kinds of things can be grown from seed in this way. One of the easiest is geranium (*Pelargonium*), and two outstanding climbers grown as annuals are *Ipomoea tricolor* 'Pearly Gates' and *Ipomoea lobata* 'Citronella.'

Propagators. If you want to get a little bit professional then perhaps you'll invest in a propagator. Some seedlings are temperamental: if conditions aren't exactly right then they won't perform. Simple propagators have a base tray that holds the seed-starting mix and a clear plastic lid and come in a range of sizes. There may be a layer of capillary matting in the bottom that you water instead of the soil mix and the water is drawn up from underneath. The lid has adjustable ventilation holes for all-important air circulation. You simply pop the seed trays or pots inside. Slightly more advanced products have a heating element in the base and you can adjust the temperature to give your seeds and seedlings the perfect environment. The whole thing costs no more than a light bulb to run.

Hardening off, planting, thinning and transplanting. Once seeds have germinated they normally require a lower temperature, which means putting them outside. They don't like the shock though, so for the first week cover them or bring them in at night. This is called "hardening off."

Don't be tempted to leave seedlings all bunched up because they'll fight for space and become weedy. It seems quite brutal but you have to thin them to whatever it says on the packet and discard the rest.

Transplanting is the same thing only you move all the plants to a different place – either into open ground, or more likely into individual, larger containers of potting or multipurpose soil mix. Hold the plant by its lowest "seed" leaves and tease it out of the mix gently with a dibber or a pencil. Make a new hole with the dibber, replant and water in.

It's not cheating. If even these simple methods make your toes curl then there is another way. More and more ready-grown seedlings or small plants are available from garden centers these

days. Sweet peas and tomatoes are two particularly good labor savers. Try not to get tempted by the tiny shrubs: they're so small that once they're in the ground you'll barely be able to see them.

Collecting and storing

This is a great way to get new plants. Collect seed from your friends' gardens or from your own. Don't whip the seed heads off plants as soon as the flowers fade. Leave them until they are ready.

As the seed pods swell and ripen, they dry out. Choose healthy-looking plants, and fix paper bags around the pods with elastic bands before cutting them off with scissors and shaking the seeds into the bag. In a cupboard, store dry seed in screw-top jars or empty film canisters, ready for planting next year. And don't forget to write the name of the seed on the jar or canister.

Self-seeders

These are my favorite. You may have to sow the seed initially or buy an established plant, but then they get on with it themselves without any encouragement.

Lady's mantle is one of the best perennials, and the evergreen *Corydalis lutea* seeds itself everywhere. Little seedlings appear all over the place: you can easily move them around (they often wilt initially but soon pick up) or just leave them be.

Foxgloves and lupines are easy as well. They're actually biennial, so flower in their second season, but if you sow seed for two successive years, you'll get flowering plants annually.

Forget-me-nots, with their little blue flowers, are outstanding. Start them off from seed and in spring either thin the clumps and transplant them to where you want them or just leave them. They're short-lived and in summer, after a long flowering, they'll have dropped their seed and you can pull them out easily. Throw the plant on the compost heap and the seeds are already germinating in the soil for next year.

An annual climber is the yellow nasturtium, *Tropaeolum peregrinum*. It's actually tender but readily grows again from seed each year. It will grow a good 10 feet up into fences or trees, producing masses of curious yellow flowers from summer to autumn before dying down in the frost. It might need a little bit of help at the beginning to get it twined onto its support.

Some bedding plants that you buy at great cost from the garden center will also start to seed themselves. The white-flowered alyssum springs up in crevices and in between plants and the annual lobelia, although not prolific, will also start to pop up unexpectedly.

Gravel paths are made far more interesting when toadflax, mullein, nasturtium and Welsh poppies seed themselves in it. Just pluck out any unwanted plants.

Honesty will grow in dark or dry places where other things won't. It forms those familiar circular, opaque seed heads.

Apart from annuals and perennials, watch out for shrubs and climbers that have self-seeded as well. *Viburnum tinus*, sweet box, passion flower and golden hop are quite usual but don't forget to move them to an appropriate location before they get too big.

The only problem with this method of gardening is remembering not to weed all the seedlings out as they emerge. You have to learn to recognize and cherish your self-seeders. And remember, unrotted mulches such as bark will hinder the success of seeds.

Cuttings

Don't be scared of taking cuttings, especially as only the simplest of methods are described here. Always use healthy, nonflowering shoots. As a general rule deciduous cuttings are more successful than evergreens. There are four different types of cutting.

Softwood tip cuttings

These are taken from the new, soft growth of a plant, in spring. Take cuttings in the morning when the plants are pumped up with water. Use sharp shears, scissors or a knife to cut a nonflowering shoot up to about 5 inches long, making a straight cut just below where some leaves join. Put it into a polyethylene bag immediately to stop it from dry-ing out. Fix a piece of netting over the top of a jar or milk bottle full of water to support the stems. Remove the bottom leaves, leaving three to five pairs, and put the stump into the jar of water – or a pot of seed starting mix, which may do just as well.

Suitable plants for softwood cuttings include a range of shrubs and climbers: abelia, abutilon, Chinese plumbago, smoke bush, fuchsia, hydrangea, geranium, mock orange and wisteria.

Semiripe cuttings

Again, use the current year's growth, but in late summer or early autumn – when shoots have started to ripen. Take about 4–6 inches of stem; the tip will be soft but the base will be a bit firm and woody. Remove the lower leaves and any side shoots, and with a knife, scrape off a 1-inch strip of bark from the base to stimulate root growth. Dip the base of the shoot in a tub of hormone rooting powder (get it from any garden center), make a hole in your soil mix with a dibber or your finger, insert about a third of the cutting and firm it in. Put a clear polyethylene bag over the top of the container as a mini-greenhouse and secure it with an elastic band. If you have a propagator, use that, but don't cover geraniums as they are prone to rotting. Put it on a windowsill and plant it outside when fully rooted. This may be the following spring, depending on how hardy the plant is.

Suitable plants for increasing when you bring them in before frosts are half-hardy perennials like geraniums (*Pelargonium*), and shrubs like Japanese laurel, camellia, silk tassel bush, photinia and skimmia. Deciduous shrubs are the best candidates, although lavender is the easiest; in September take 6-inch cuttings, rub off the lower leaves and stick them straight into the ground. The success rate is very high.

Hardwood cuttings

Hardwood cuttings are just that: a hard, woody piece of stem from the current year's growth with any soft bits removed. Take 4–6-inch cuttings from midautumn to early winter. Deciduous plants will be leafless by that time but remove the lower leaves of evergreens and don't bury any leaves underground. The top of the cutting should be cut at an angle just above a bud. Dig a small "V" shaped trench or a hole and put some coarse sand (from a garden center or supply yard) in the bottom. Place the cutting in the hole or trench and lean it against the side. Backfill with earth so that about an inch sticks out the top. It can take over a year for them to root so you need to put them somewhere undisturbed like at the back of a border. There isn't any maintenance. Dogwood, mock orange, spiraea and viburnums are good for this.

Use deciduous hardwood cuttings to mark rows of vegetables: just cut them and shove them in the ground. If they root, all well and good.

Root cuttings

This is the best way for perennials that can't be divided easily: drumstick primroses, bear's breeches, Japanese anemones, phlox, globeflower, mullein, sea holly and ornamental thistles.

In spring or autumn, dig up your plant (or just some roots from older specimens) and select some healthy roots. They should be about 2 inches thick. Take a knife and make a straight cut at the plant end of a root and make a sloping cut at the other end. Move down the root and take as many root cuttings as you can; the length will depend on the particular plant but 2–6 inches is a rough guide. Remove any lateral roots. Put cuttings in a bag to keep them moist until you use them. Prepare a seed tray of sterile soil mix. Insert the cuttings, slanty cut downwards, and top up with mix so that the tips are just showing. Cover with an inch of horticultural sand if you want. Put on a windowsill in autumn or put it outside on the deck in spring. Keep the cuttings watered.

Dividing plants

Clumps

Hundreds of perennials, from salvias to euphorbia, can be divided. If the plant has lots of shoots coming from the base and it has lots of roots, then it's probably suitable. The time to do it is late autumn or spring when it's not too cold. It's very easy.

Get a fork or spade, dig all around the plant and lift it out of the ground. Some plants like hostas have a solid core and these are best cut into smaller lumps with a sharp spade or knife. Old kitchen knives are good. Each new piece of plant should have at least one shoot and some roots attached to it.

Other species that are a mass of roots and stems such as geranium or daylily can be prized apart with a fork. If you've got two forks this is really easy. Slide the prongs into and through the heart of the plant, forks back to back. Pull the handles together, push apart and pull together. The plant easily splits into two. Younger, smaller plants may be teased apart with your fingers. Replant and water them in.

Other good plants for division include yarrow, astilbe, campanula, tickseed, hellebores, catmint, New Zealand flax, coneflower, Chinese rhubarb, sedum and globeflower.

Rhizomes

Certain plants, including some iris, grow from a swollen stem or rhizome that is visible on the soil surface, and these plants can also be divided. Lift a clump and, with a knife, cut away the newer rhizomes from the old ones. Cut the ends cleanly and trim the leaves to about 6 inches. Replant them so that half the rhizome is visible, the roots are in the soil and the foliage is upright.

Runners and offsets

Some "parent" plants such as strawberries send out runners, which are basically babies attached to the parent plant by a sort of umbilical cord. They can be detached and replanted once they have rooted. You can do this at any time during the growing season but avoid the heat of the day because the roots will shrivel. Ideally the new plants should be replanted in a cool spot out of direct sunlight; water well to establish. To encourage rooting, the new plants can be pegged down with "U" shaped pieces of wire before they're detached from the parent plant. Other plants that produce little baby offsets include camomile and succulents like American aloe. *Sempervivum* don't even need to root before you take them off.

Bulbs

You should lift crowded bulbs like crocus and daffodil during the dormant season. (Snowdrops particularly like to be divided and transplanted in the spring after they've flowered.) Every few years is about right – but more than likely you'll dig them up by mistake. Don't just bury them again but divide them, remove the offsets and replant in irregular groups (see *Getting Planted*). Small bulbs probably won't flower in the first year.

birds, bees and salamanders

Your garden is more than a refuge for people and plants: it can provide food, shelter and breeding sites for a whole host of animals, most of which are welcome. Of thousands of species of insect in the U.S., fewer than one percent are garden pests, and of the remainder, many act as beneficial pollinators or as predators and parasites of pests. With the careful planting and management of a garden you can encourage a wide range of wildlife. Salamanders, frogs and toads are beneficial residents of any garden and their presence is a good indication of a healthy environment. A pretty little pond will attract these ancient creatures, and birds will welcome it, too.

In a very simple view of a naturally occurring food chain . . . the plants feed the animals; the animals manure the ground; the manure feeds the soil; the soil feeds the plants; and on and on. Because of the demands we put on a garden, we have to supplement the manure with extra feeds – and because a garden is essentially artificial, we need to lend a helping hand to the wildlife by specifically planting species to provide food and breeding grounds. In order to do this properly we have to provide flowers and berries all year round. A gap could leave insects and other animals without food, kill them off and break the chain. This organic philosophy maintains a balance of both predators and pests.

Things you want

Butterflies

You can easily encourage butterflies into your garden by planting a succession of flowering species throughout the warm months: primrose, cowslip, forget-me-not, honesty and yellow flag for the spring, followed by thrift, thyme, mallow, honeysuckle, catmint, cornflower, ox-eye daisy, marjoram, lavender, veronica, sea holly, bugle, corncockle, Buddleja and *Sedum spectabile*. Red admiral, small tortoiseshell, and peacocks (and ladybugs) like some stinging nettles for breeding. Grow the nettles in a tub to stop them spreading everywhere.

Bees

Bees will help to pollinate your flowers, fruit and vegetables. They're an essential in a garden and rarely sting, so don't be a wimp – get some in your garden. They like bergamot, foxglove, globe thistle, penstemon, broom and similar plants to those enjoyed by butterflies.

You can make or buy an insect house, which is like a very small open-fronted bird box with a sloping roof to keep out the rain. Put it near flowering plants or water, off the ground but not too high up and stack a load of hollow plant stems or short bamboo sticks into it. This will be a perfect home for solitary bees and ladybugs.

Hover flies

The larvae of many hover flies eat aphids and you can encourage them by planting marigolds and nasturtiums. Many other predators can be introduced or encouraged in your garden. See *Pestilence and Disease.*

Birds

Birds can be a pain but they can also be an asset to any garden and worth sacrificing a few apples and berries for. They eat grubs, caterpillars, slugs and aphids, so you should go out of your way to entice them.

Over recent years, many birds have adapted to an urban life and the population in gardens has soared as people buy high-quality wild-bird food and plant berry-laden species that feed the birds during the crucial winter months. There has been an explosion in some species such as greater spotted wood-pecker, bluejay, goldfinch and sparrowhawk as they take advantage of the shelter provided by buildings and smaller gardens.

If you've got a cat then you'll have to be careful about attracting birds and where you put the bird feeder, or you may inadvertently save some money on pet food.

To encourage nesting, put bird boxes around the garden – different-sized boxes and apertures for different birds. You can even get one to fix in the eaves for house martins, who eat thousands of fly-ing insects every day. Natural nest sites are provided by hedges and climbers like *Clematis montana*, but be careful not to disturb the birds or prune plants too late in the summer when they're nesting.

Dead wood should normally be removed from trees to prevent fungal diseases but if it can be left or stacked in a pile, well away from your house, it will be teeming with insects and be a rich food source for woodpeckers and other birds.

A bird bath or a pond is an essential source of drinking and bathing water throughout the year, but do try and get something a little nicer than those hideous concrete ones. Be innovative, even if it's only an old half-barrel.

Pigeons can be a menace in towns, leaving little presents on your car and on the roof. Get rid of roosting sites where possible; in extreme cases the Yellow Pages can list the answer under Pest Control.

Put netting over certain cherries and other fruit susceptible to bird attack. Fix it firmly to the ground so birds don't get entangled in it. Criss-crosses of black cotton keep them away from crocus – especially the yellow ones, which they seem to like best – but all these precautions are unsightly and awkward, and the best bet is to plant enough to share. Trial and error.

Pond life

If you do only one thing in a garden to attract wildlife, make it a pond. It doesn't have to be enormous. A half barrel sunk into the ground is a start but if you make it bigger it will become a balanced ecosystem and can virtually look after itself. Butyl rubber is the best liner and can be used for any size or shape (get it from fish pond specialists and some garden centers). Ideally, put it in some sun and away from trees that will drop thousands of leaves into it. Water is the breeding ground for frogs, toads and salamanders, which devour slugs and other pests. Bear in mind that goldfish eat tadpoles and insect life, so should be left out of a true wildlife pond. Be sure to have at least one shallow bit at the edge so that birds and animals can drink and bathe; and so all the amphibious things, which basically just breed in the water, can get out and do all their other stuff on dry land. Dragonflies and damselflies love plants that stick out of the water, such as iris and arrow-head. Essential waterborne oxygenating plants like hornwort and milfoil are better than rampant Canadian pondweed, and floaters like water lilies provide important shade.

Do think carefully, though, if you have small children because ponds, however shallow, can be death traps.

Honeybees

Keeping a beehive is a complete and fascinating hobby by itself, but the domestic honeybee is a gentle creature that can work wonders for a garden. Flowers, fruit and vegetables will all do better if there is a beehive nearby. Honeybees are all female except for a few males, called drones, which do nothing but loll around and eat all day. Besides the benefit for your plants, there's a sweet bonus – the honey. If keeping bees is more than you want to deal with, try to find a local beekeeper who will agree to put one of his hives in your yard. You might even get some free honey out of the deal.

Bats

Bats can eat up to 500 flying insects an hour and they do no harm, so welcome them with open arms. They don't fly into your hair either; that's a myth. Fix a bat-house to a tree. Bats enter from beneath and rest on a series of vertical bunk beds, and their voracious appetites will more than repay your hospitality.

Centipedes, millipedes and beetles

These thrive if given plenty of ground cover and a chemical-free, organic garden. They eat lots of insects and slugs.

Things you might not want

Squirrels

Several squirrel-resistant bird feeders are available to keep the lovable rogues away from the seed but most of these devices also deny access to anything larger than a sparrow. Curry-flavored bird seed is becoming available now. The birds can't taste the curry and the squirrels don't enjoy Delhi belly.

On the other hand, you may not consider them a problem at all, and it may not bother you that they dig up the lawn to use as a pantry. There's not too much that you can do about it anyway – apart

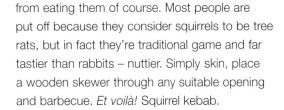

top to bottom
Bee
Ladybug
Wasps

top to bottom
Cowslip
Butterfly
Marigold

top to bottom
Beetles
Ivy
Berries

from eating them of course. Most people are put off because they consider squirrels to be tree rats, but in fact they're traditional game and far tastier than rabbits – nuttier. Simply skin, place a wooden skewer through any suitable opening and barbecue. *Et voilà!* Squirrel kebab.

The urban fox

Foxes are still on the increase but don't pose any real problem. They are wary of cats and certainly won't attack, but they do have a propensity to rummage through your garbage and spread it all over the street.

Mice

Mice aren't really a problem but they sometimes nibble at your strawberries and rob the larger seeds like peas and beans. Use humane traps and release them a long way away – or get a cat.

Deer

Fairly shy and not often seen, deer live in the country and on the edge of suburbia so if your garden backs onto open land, a golf course, or woodland, you might get nighttime visitors. Perhaps you'll never see them but some of your flowers will disappear. Either kiss your roses goodbye or put up a 10-foot deer fence.

Raccoons

People have tried lights, blaring radios and electric fences, but raccoons are smarter than most people and usually win out.

Rabbits

Rabbits munch lots of things right to the ground. There is only one solution: Erect a special rabbit fence to keep them out.

Rules of Thumb

— Informal, mixed hedges provide better, undisturbed nesting sites and a richer source of flowers and berries than neatly clipped barriers.

— Grow plenty of trees and shrubs, particularly native varieties like mountain ash, silver birch, crab apples and cherries. Ivy is a good nest site but also provides a valuable autumn source of nectar for insects.

— Generally, flowering plants are an important source of nectar and pollen for bees, butterflies and other insects. Avoid double-flowered forms, which often have less pollen. Some wildflowers, like buttercups, poppies and clover, can hold their own against cultivated and exotic plants. Grow these in your garden, particularly local species.

— Be tolerant of some damage to crops and ornamentals and don't be tempted to use chemicals.

— Compost heaps, while essential to an organic garden, also provide a happy home for worms and a host of other insects.

— Don't get too anal about your lawn. Let it grow a bit longer so that things like clover can flower to attract butterflies and other insects – and what's more, it won't go brown so fast during dry periods.

— Leave seedheads on flowers, *Sedum* and sunflower for example, as food for birds. It's a good excuse not to be excessively tidy in the garden and dead vegetation provides a winter home for insects.

— Feed birds only in the cold winter months. At other times of the year there should be plenty of natural food around for them.

fruit, vegetables and herbs

Growing your own fruit and vegetables is wondrous. It's not about saving money, it's about the delights of being able to pop into the garden or reach out to the windowsill for a handful of cilantro or tomatoes.

Some things are more labor intensive than others and it really is a case of you reap what you sow. I could go into extraordinary detail about double-digging and soil conditioners, but in the tradition and work ethic of this book, I'm giving you the "just try it," simplest version of events.

And everything here is organic. If you want perfect-looking, chemically enhanced specimens, you can go shopping – but at the possible expense of a few leaves, your own produce will taste fantastic and be as pure as the driven snow, or rather, unadulterated by sprayed horrors.

Before you plant anything, you need to decide what you want to grow, how much of it you want and how much time you're prepared to spend on it. These edible crops are generally easy and don't need constant attention once they're growing, apart from a little feeding, some water and the occasional tweak. As a general rule, vegetables, herbs and fruit need to be grown in plenty of sun in a fairly fertile soil with some shelter from the wind. There can be problems, in which case check out the *Pestilence and Disease* section, but on the whole, just sit back and see what happens. And while it's very satisfying growing stuff from seed, it is OK to cheat and buy ready-germinated seedlings or established young plants from the garden centers.

Instead of creating a special vegetable garden, you can include edible stuff among the ornamentals. Pole beans can be grown up trellises or over an arbor – the flowers, and subsequently the beans, providing just as much color and interest as any passion flower. Parsley and other herbs can be grown in terracotta pots, and the globular flowers of onions and the brilliant leaves of ruby chard can cheer up the gloomiest corner. Special tomato and strawberry varieties can be grown in hanging baskets, and lettuce is quite happy in a window box. By slotting the vegetables into the other planting you're automatically companion planting (see *Pestilence and Disease*), providing a haven for the predators that will control the bugs that would otherwise ravage your crop.

Organic gardening is about trial and error, so if something doesn't work in your particular patch, grow something that does work. You'll probably need to fork in some compost and scatter a bit of fertilizer around but don't worry too much about the pH thing.

Vegetables

Seeds
Vegetable seeds are available at garden centers, or you can buy them by mail order from a catalog. The time to start sowing is in the spring, on your windowsill during the frosts (see *Grow Your Own*) and outside in the ground once it is warmer. For a constant supply, sow seeds at intervals so that you get a continuous harvest.

Before you sow outside, rake in a couple of handfuls of fish, blood and bonemeal fertilizer per square yard and fork in about 2 inches of well-rotted compost. Very poor soils may need a bit more work.

For first-time sowers the major seed companies produce strips of tape with the seed prespaced and sown. It doesn't get much easier than laying them out, covering with soil and watering.

Seedlings are very hard to distinguish in their early stages and it is possible to accidentally remove your vegetables and just leave the weeds. To avoid this it's a good idea to prepare the seed bed and then allow it to lie empty for a couple of weeks. This allows dormant weed seeds to germinate so you can remove them immediately prior to sowing. Your new seedlings will be one step ahead of any future weeds and identification becomes easy.

Seeds and seedlings will need watering fairly regularly in dry weather.

To start seedlings indoors, sow them in seed trays on the windowsill or in propagators.

Now turn to page 125 in *Grow Your Own* to see what to do next!

Cold frame. This is like an unheated mini-greenhouse. You can buy one ready-made, or make one from an old storm window and some 2 x 10 lumber nailed together for the base. A couple of hinges are nice, but not essential. You use a cold frame to harden off baby seedlings, plant flats of seeds earlier than you could in the open, and even keep stuff going into the winter. A cold frame is a terrific tool.

Some ground rules

The deep-bed system. Most things here can be grown in pots but if you want a vegetable patch you can make even the smallest area rich in nutrients and accessible with this system. The basic idea is to dig deep, fork over the bottom of your hole, throw in loads of organic matter and fill the hole back up. This will make roots go down, not across, so you can grow more plants with a bigger yield in a smaller area.

Crop rotation. This can get a bit complicated with different vegetables belonging to different groups. So, to avoid confusion, follow this basic principle: Don't grow the same thing in the same place in consecutive years because it tires the soil and lowers the resistance to pests and disease. Keep things moving.

Pinching out

This is a general and fantastic rule of gardening and you can try it on any plant you like. If you pinch out the new, growing tips, you channel the plant's energy into the lower growth so you get stronger, bushier specimens with larger (although fewer) flowers and fruit. Remove about 2 inches of shoot tip with thumbnail and forefinger.

Garlic

Very easy to grow in a sunny spot and, for an added bonus, garlic has attractive leaves and flowers. At first buy the bulbs from a garden center

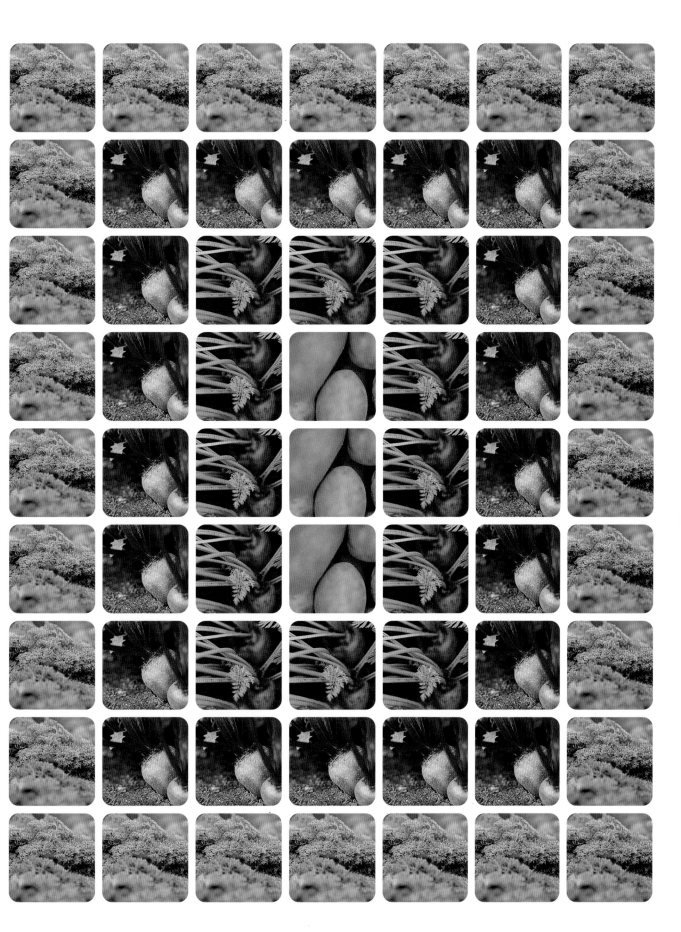

or seed catalog and then in subsequent years simply replant your own stock by separating the cloves and planting them pointy end up in autumn or early spring. Make holes about 1 inch deep and 6 inches apart. Except for a bit of weeding they're virtually maintenance free. Harvest in summer when the leaves go yellow, clean the bulbs and dry them in the sun before stringing them together and storing them in a cool, dark, frost-free place.

Onions

Grow a reliable type like the yellow 'New York Early' or liven up your salads with the aptly named 'Redman.' You can buy sets, which are just small bulbs, in the spring. Plant them so you can just see the tops, 4 to 6 inches apart, and expect to get about 3 to 4 pounds per square yard. Harvest them when the leaves are yellow and they look the right size. Scallions can be sown from February onwards or in August and September to grow through the winter, ready for harvesting in late spring.

Carrots

There's nothing like pulling your own fresh carrots from the soil. They're very easy to grow, packed with vitamin A and good for your skin. Carrots can be sown in succession using different varieties to produce throughout the year. Start sowing them in spring and then thin them out to about 2 inches when they're large enough to handle. Remove weeds by hoeing and drag some soil on to the "shoulders" of the carrots to stop them from going green. Harvest while young. Short varieties are good for growing in containers.

Potatoes

Different varieties do well in different areas and they prefer a soil that is acid, moist and rich in organic matter. Use disease-free seed potatoes. Cut them into pieces, making sure you have an "eye" on every piece. Plant them about 4 inches deep and a foot apart. When they're about 8 inches tall scatter a couple of handfuls of fish, blood and bonemeal per square yard.

Potatoes often grow just under the soil surface so mound up earth against the stems to stop them turning green and poisonous. Early varieties like 'Norland' can be harvested as you need them once the plants start flowering. 'Kennebec' is good for heavier and poorer soils and withstands drought well.

Eggplants

Early types are best because they crop for longer. 'Orient Express' is good and a white variety called 'Osterei' will let you know why they're called eggplants. Sow inside in March or April on a windowsill in polystyrene cells and transfer to 4-inch pots when large enough to handle. Harden them off in a cold frame or plant out in April or May, 18 inches apart in a deep bed in full sun. Alternatively, buy ready-grown plants. They can be grown in large pots in a sunny spot on the patio. Eggplants flourish if grown next to tarragon and thyme. Pinch out the growing tip at 10 inches, stake main stem firmly and tie side shoots to the canes. Remove any extra flowers when about five fruits per plant are swelling and apply liquid fertilizer weekly from May. Cut in late summer when they're very shiny and ripe.

Peppers

These perform better than eggplants in colder areas but still benefit from cold frames or unheated greenhouses. 'Ace' is a sweet pepper that lives up to its name; for warmer climates or in a greenhouse 'Super Serrano' is a hot chile. These need shelter, sun and a cold frame to start. Sow on the windowsill in January or February and when they're big enough to handle transfer to 4-inch pots and then pot into larger containers as the roots fill the pots. Plant out into deep beds in about May in staggered rows, 18 inches apart or plant into final 10-inch pots. At 6 inches pinch out the growing tip. Water regularly and feed with liquid seaweed; feed outside plants weekly and feed greenhouse plants at every watering. Pick sweet peppers when they're plump and hot peppers when red or green and dry them in the sun for storing.

Tomatoes

These can be bought as bush or upright climbing types and varieties do differ enormously in flavor. 'Big Beef' lives up to its name, 'Northern Exposure' does well in cool climates, and 'Brandywine' is reputed to be the best-tasting salad tomato. 'Super Sweet 100' is a prolific cherry tomato, and 'Bellstar' is a favorite early plum tomato for canning or salad use. You can grow them from seed quite easily but it's far simpler to buy established plants. They need a sunny spot with a well-manured soil. Plant out in deep beds 18 inches apart in May with canes for climbing varieties or you can plant straight into large pots. Climbing varieties should be tied in to vertical strings and the side shoots removed from each leaf joint while still small. Remove bottom leaves as they turn yellow, and pinch out the tops after three or four trusses of fruit have formed or when they reach the top of the greenhouse. Feed weekly with liquid seaweed. Pick when ripe.

Zucchini, squashes and pumpkins

Squash vegetables need a slightly acid soil. Sow seed in the ground after the last frosts or earlier in pots on the windowsill.

Zucchini are famously heavy producers so don't plant too many. 'Condor' gives early, glossy dark green fruits, and 'Gold Rush' is deep yellow. To save space you can train them up a trellis or netting. Pick 'em young.

Summer squash come in all shapes. 'Peter Pan' is a prize-winning scallop squash, and 'Sunburst' is a vigorous patty pan type. Winter squash are good keepers, and 'Table Ace' is a good acorn type, while 'Waltham Butternut' actually tastes better three months after harvest. If the kids want a Halloween pumpkin, try 'Dill's Atlantic Giant,' which can grow up to 100 pounds or even more.

French beans

Cucumbers

'Burpless Tasty Green' is a good climbing cucumber and apparently easy to digest and 'Lemon' produces many small, round, yellow-skinned fruits. Sow on the windowsill in April, two seeds each to a 4-inch pot, and then thin to the stronger seedling after germination. Transplant about 2 feet apart in late May and grow up bamboo wigwams or trellises. Alternatively, after the frosts, sow directly into the ground in their final positions. Tie in the plants often and wind them onto the canes carefully. Pinch out the tips when they reach the tops. Feed with liquid seaweed or animal manure fertilizer every two weeks. Water frequently and harvest regularly to encourage more.

Pole beans

Pole beans can be treated as productive ornamentals and used to cover fences and trellises in a warm position out of the wind. Whatever you use as support, whether it's wires, poles or a traditional wigwam of bamboo canes, you must put it up before sowing so you don't damage the seedlings. Sow directly into the ground about 6 inches apart after the last frosts in spring. Allow two plants per cane or whatever. 'Fortex' produces long, stringless pods, and 'Kentucky Blue' is a cross between two old favorites. Help the plants twine round their supports and nip the tips out when they reach the top. Watering frequently while flowering helps pollination and mulching is useful to retain moisture. Pick continuously from about the end of July while the beans are still young and not too stringy. Expect about 6 pounds per square yard of ground.

Sweet corn

It takes up a fair bit of space and each plant produces only one or two cobs but the taste makes it worthwhile. Seed is sown directly into the ground in early or mid-May. One plant every 10 inches in a block helps wind pollination, and mulching and watering during flowering are important to boost growth. Corn can be harvested and eaten immediately when the tassels turn brown, from July to October depending on variety. A dab of vegetable oil on the silks helps keep worms away.

French beans

These may be dwarf, or climbers that need some support. Either way, they're ideal for containers. 'Triomphe de Farcy' is a classic filet bean. 'Tavera' and 'Maxibel' are long and stringless. Grow them like pole beans.

Peas

Sow from March to May in succession to avoid a single harvest – about ten plants per square foot should do it – and cover with 1½ to 2 inches of soil. They will need supporting with pea netting or sticks. Pick them when they're still young and as close to cooking as possible, then cut the foliage off but leave the roots in the ground because they produce nitrogen. Sugar Snap' is a good wilt-resistant variety and 'Oregon Giant' is a good snow pea.

Broccoli

Sow the seed directly into the ground in shallow holes, enough to get one plant every 10 inches. Successional sowings can be made from late March to early July for harvesting from early summer into autumn. A very fast grower like 'Green Comet' produces good heads only 55 days after sowing. Soil may need liming to raise the pH to above 6.5 but avoid sandy and shallow soils and water regularly.

Salad

Salad crops can be harvested all year if given protection. They can be grown as "catch crops," that is, tucked in among others or put in window boxes or any other available space.

Lettuce

A succession of lettuces can be harvested from May to October by sowing a little seed every two weeks from early March to early July in a soil that doesn't dry out totally. A semishaded spot will be all right. Sow in rows just over $\frac{1}{4}$ inch deep and when the plants are large enough to handle, thin to 6 to 10 inches apart in blocks. Early sowings can be protected in a cold frame and planted out at intervals as a succession crop. Water as they grow and watch out for slugs. Cut whole leaves or pick whole lettuces complete with stalks. 'Crispino' can be used to produce the familiar iceberg lettuce, which doesn't have to be picked as soon as it's ready. 'Royal Oak Leaf' looks great in the garden and tastes great from the salad bowl. 'Lollo Rossa' has excellent frilly red leaves. Lettuces are normally ready for harvest after about ten weeks, but you can cut young leaves well before that.

Arugula

Sow shallowly in spring and then every four weeks. Harvest by cutting leaves with scissors, leaving a bit of plant behind to grow on. The older the plants the more peppery they get.

Watercress

Shady, moist soil is essential for growing water-cress. Dig a trench a foot deep and half fill with compost or manure; fill the rest up with soil. Alternatively, grow in pots and stand in water, which must be changed daily. Watercress can be grown from seed, but it's easiest to root cuttings from bought watercress in water and then plant out in May. Water copiously, pinch out the shoot tips and remove flowers. Cut as you need it. Pests and disease are not a problem.

Swiss chard

This leafy vegetable not only tastes good but it looks fantastic as well. Ruby chard (a variety) has brilliant red veins that stand out against the green of the leaf. It's ideal for a border and outstanding in pots. Rich, moisture-retentive soils are best, and you may need to add a bit of lime.

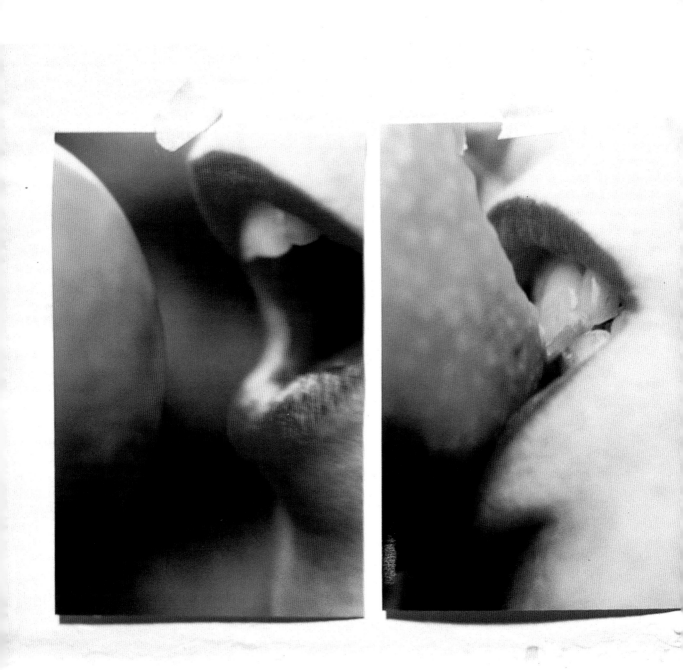

Sow in April, two or three seeds to each 1-inch-deep hole and then thin to the strongest seedling – sow more in July for the winter when they can withstand the frost. For container-grown plants, first sow into 4-inch pots and then pot into the final container, where they will need a fair amount of water. Harvest by pulling outer leaves off, leaving the remaining plant to grow on.

Radishes

There are two types of radish: the familiar red, or red and white salad types such as 'Sparkler' and 'French Breakfast,' and the longer, often white, tap-roots sold as daikon, such as 'Miyashige.' They all tolerate a wide range of soil conditions, though they prefer a bit of shade and moisture. All are ideal to grow among other plants. Sow in succession from late winter under cold frames and then unprotected until midautumn. Scatter the seed thinly in wide shallow bands, water if the soil is dry and remove weeds. Thinning isn't necessary but harvest regularly before they get fibrous and woody.

Herbs

Herbs generally prefer a sunny, well-drained, light soil, so dig deep or fork in sand. Many are from Mediterranean regions and actually thrive on poor, well-drained soil, making them ideal, because they don't need much watering or feeding or anything. Adding lime or spent mushroom compost to an acidic soil raises the pH to the preferred, but not essential, 7.0 to 7.5.

As a general rule, cut herbs before they flower, taking care not to damage the leaves and lose essential oils. Hang them upside down in an airy place to dry and then crumble them into jars for storage; or just hang from the kitchen ceiling. Ideally grow them near the kitchen, next to the deck or in raised beds to get the full benefit of their scent.

French tarragon

Does wonders for chicken but use sparingly. Grow plants a foot apart in a well-drained sunny soil. It's a perennial so it lasts forever but to maintain the flavor, divide every four years or so. Pick the fresh leaves all season and dry spring-cut ones for a stronger flavor.

Basil

Sweet basil is the one to grow – perfect for salads and most Italian food. A tender annual, this is best sown on the windowsill and planted out after frosts and then succession sown all summer. You can buy growing plants; space them at 10 inches. Keep plants well watered and pick leaves all summer, but remove flowers as they appear or that will be the end of your crop. Use it fresh, freeze it, make a batch of pesto, or pack in a jar and cover with olive oil for the winter.

Cilantro

An absolute essential with fish and curries, or just to brighten up scrambled eggs at breakfast time. It's easy to grow this annual from seed. Succession sow, keep cutting and pinch off flowers. Ideal for pots, window boxes or sown directly into the ground.

Chives

A small, low-growing member of the onion clan that can't fail given a bit of sun. Grow *in situ* from seed or, more simply, dig up a piece of someone else's clump in spring or autumn. The pink flower heads make it a good plant for the front of the border or in a pot. Divide the clumps of small bulbs whenever you get around to it and cut right back every now and then. Harvest with a pair of scissors and snip into salads. It doesn't dry well but can be frozen in ice cubes.

Mint

If you're not careful, you can end up with a garden half full of mint; its spreading roots know no bounds. To keep it contained, plant it in an old bucket sunk into the ground or keep in a well-watered pot. Applemint and spearmint are the best for cooking and the former resists the rust disease that can make a plant ugly. It prefers a bit of shade and is easily grown from root cuttings or by dividing established plants. Pick regularly and freeze the leaves for storing.

Dill

Popular in Scandinavian and Russian cooking, with a taste somewhere between parsley and fennel, this feathery herb is perfect with potatoes, fish and with yogurt and sour cream. Sow seeds outside in a sunny, well-drained site and thin to a foot apart or buy established plants. Water

well in dry weather and pick the leaves as needed.

Parsley

Surrounded by superstition, parsley allegedly grows best where the wife wears the trousers, and you're not meant to transplant it because it's said to cause misery and even death to the recipient. Grow it from seed in midspring and then midsummer. Harvest regularly by scissor trimming and grow in pots indoors on the windowsill for the winter.

Rosemary

Lovely with lamb, and you can grow it as a shrub among other ornamentals, or even as a path edging or small hedge. The evergreen leaves and pale blue flowers make it a good choice next to a patio in the sun. Trim back the shoots by about one-third after flowering to keep bushes healthy and compact. It can be grown from cuttings (see *Grow Your Own*) or you can buy established plants and put in well-drained soil.

Oregano

Nobody can seem to agree whether oregano and marjoram are different plants or not. Whatever the truth, plant as young or divided plants a foot apart in sunny, well-drained soil. They make rather pleasing green mounds, at home in the border or in pots: Golden marjoram has bright yellow-green leaves. Pinch out the tips, trim with shears or just harvest regularly to keep the plants bushy and neat and then cut back in late autumn to about 2 inches above ground. It can be dried or frozen for storage.

Basil

Thyme

The many different varieties of thyme include creeping plants like *Thymus serpyllum,* suitable for growing in the gaps among paving, or the bushier *T. vulgaris* types, some of which have variegated leaves, and the yellow, lemon-scented thyme *T.* x *citriodorus.* Take cuttings or divide the plants in summer. An annual scattering of lime and the addition of sand can make the difference between a glorious and an ugly plant. Trim regularly with shears and cut back after flowering to keep plants bushy. Mounding soil into the center of leggy plants to encourage new shoots can rejuvenate neglected specimens.

Fruit

Fruit trees

Buy one- or two-year-old plants in autumn, either pot grown or with bare roots, and plant like ornamentals. Dig deep and include plenty of compost. Look near the bottom of the trunk for a grafted "knuckle." This should be 4 to 6 inches above the soil level. Mulching is a good idea.

Feed in spring by scattering two handfuls per square yard of fish, blood and bonemeal but not too close to the trunk where it is useless. Mulch annually with compost or manure.

Watering for an hour a day in dry weather helps the fruit to swell as it grows. If you want to get bigger fruit, thin each cluster by removing the central fruits in midsummer.

Most fruit trees need to be pollinated by another tree in order to produce fruit, though some are self-pollinating. The other tree may be in your garden or your neighbor's garden: The bees do all the hard work. When you're buying new fruit trees, the pollinating group number (which relates to the time of year it flowers) should be on the label. You need another plant in the same group or one on either side, so follow the advice of your nursery.

Cherries

The sweet cherry 'Star Stella' and the more acid-tasting 'Montmorency' are self-pollinating and therefore ideal for the small garden because you need only the one tree. The birds always get to them, especially sweet ones, before you do – so if you want to save the crop, you ought to cover it with netting. This is much easier to do if the trees are fan trained flat against a wall or fence. South-facing walls are best for the sweet types but acid varieties will grow in shade. Standards and bushes need very little pruning and they'll fruit after the first four or five years.

Apples

Apple trees grow easily, fruit for up to thirty years and can be trained into any shape. They need a sunny, sheltered spot and pollinating by a different variety in order to crop properly, but even crab apples can provide this service. They start fruiting after two years and the fruit is ripe when it comes off easily. The choice of varieties is endless.

Fig

'Brown Turkey' and 'Celeste' are pretty hardy but a hot summer is needed for a good, well-ripened crop. They must be grown in a south-facing spot as bushes or, more suitably, against a wall as a sort of fan. No special pruning is needed. The most important thing is to restrict the roots by planting in a 3-foot-square hole, 2 feet deep. Put rubble in the bottom and concrete slabs or bricks up the sides. Refill with soil and compost or manure. Thin the branches in summer, letting the sun in to ripen the fruit and remove several old branches and any remaining large fruit in winter. They can be grown in pots and moved inside for winter but you need to water well.

Strawberry

Large summer fruiting plants have the tastiest strawberries. There are tons of varieties, but 'Sparkle' and 'Honeoye' are among the best. A moist, well-drained soil in a sunny spot is essential. Plant in late summer about a foot apart and be careful not to plant too deeply. Water well. Planting through black plastic or strawberry mats eliminates weeds and protects the fruit. Using straw also deters slugs. Alternatively, grow in traditional terracotta strawberry pots, window boxes or hanging baskets. Alpine strawberries can even be trained around hoops. After harvesting, feed the plants with potash and, every four years, dump them and put new plants in a new location.

Grapes

'Interlaken Seedless' is a delicious green table grape, and 'Canadice' is the best of the red varieties. They love poor soil in the sun and should be grown against a south-facing wall, 6 feet apart on horizontal wires. Plant in the autumn with well-rotted compost or manure (they like a bit of nutrition for their first two years) and train the shoots horizontally; the fruiting stems grow vertically from these. Thin the bunches to allow the fruits to swell. Grapes can be picked from new vines after two years once the stems have turned from green to brown.

Blackberries and other berries

Blackberry, raspberry, gooseberry, red currant, black currant, elderberry – all prefer a moist but well-drained soil in sun or light shade. When you plant, prune to 6 inches tall and then restrain new growth between horizontal wires. They grow up to about 10 feet wide. The fruit grows on last year's wood so train all of the first year's growth up one side of the main stem and the following year, train the branches up the other side. The first crop will be in one or two years; and after harvest, prune the fruited canes to ground level. Mulch in late winter.

Kiwi

These hairy fruits can be trained against a wall or on horizontal wires. Often a male and a female plant are needed to produce fruit although 'Issai' is self-pollinating. Grow in sun in a fertile soil but shelter from winds and avoid frost-prone areas. In early spring prune sideshoots to leave three or four buds, creating a permanent framework. Pests and disease are generally not a problem.

containers

For people with only a windowsill or a small deck, containers may be the only way they can garden. Containers are a perfect way of gardening in the microclimate of towns and cities where they brighten and soften hard urban lines, and allow you to be creative and have a lot of control over what's going on.

The key to successful container gardening is to choose the right pot, the right soil mix and the right plants. Water, feed and deadhead regularly and you've got it licked.

Choice of plants

Try to use some interesting plants. Bedding plants, such as lobelia and petunias, are good value but there's so much more out there – top shrubs include cabbage and other palms, topiary specimens, *Carex* and other ornamental grasses, Japanese aralia, skimmia, *Choisya* 'Aztec Pearl', America aloe and oleander. Avoid Japanese laurel, which tends to get blackened and stunted leaves in a pot.

Good perennials and annuals are euphorbias (the stars of the show), bear's breeches, *Sedum*, marguerites, geraniums and all the plants I recommend for window boxes and baskets.

Shrubs, trees and climbers can all be grown in pots, where you can manipulate the growing conditions – useful for growing acid-loving plants if your soil isn't suitable: Camellias and rhododendrons are appropriate. Remember, though, to water and feed regularly, or they'll struggle. In fact camellias will shed all their flower buds the following year if you don't water them right.

If you grow herbs in containers, you may want a base of permanent plants like thyme and an upright rosemary. Annual or short-lived herbs such as basil can be grown in separate pots sunk into the soil mix so that they can be replaced easily. All herbs need good drainage so add some sand to the soil mix. Other edible stuff can be grown in containers as well. Strawberries are good and salad crops like arugula, lettuce and radish can be grown among other things in a window box. The tomato variety 'Tumbler' is perfect for hanging baskets. Fruit trees on dwarf rootstocks are suitable for large pots and the 'Bing' cherry or 'Garden Gold' peach are ideal. Don't forget to water regularly when the fruit is swelling.

Containers

Depending on the quality of your neighborhood, there's a good chance that anything you put outside the front of your house is going to get stolen in a planned attack or some sort of adolescent shenanigans. There are a few ways to combat this: lighting in the front of the house is good; gravel makes the thief's approach quite noisy; and spiky plants make the getaway unpleasant. Some people cement pots into the ground or stake them with a metal pole sticking out of the bottom. Smearing Vaseline or grease all round the top makes them hard to pick up.

Geranium

Points to remember:

— Make sure your container's big enough – not only do small pots dry out quickly but you should also allow for growth.

— Shrubs and climbers never flourish as well as they would in open ground. Sometimes it may be better to put a plant into the ground. This is especially true for climbers against house walls.

— Put containers together in groups of different shapes and sizes. Odd numbers always look best. Put them at the side of steps; use them as focal points to hide ugly things or on either side of an entrance to highlight it.

— Age stoneware and terracotta by painting them with yogurt. This encourages the growth of mold and algae, which are harmless to plants.

Inside the container

Soil mix. Use multipurpose or potting mixes available from any garden center. Peat-based mixes are good but not all that sound because peat is mined from ancient wetlands.

Vermiculite. This is a slightly spongy compost additive that lightens it up, eases root penetration and holds water and therefore nutrients, making them more readily available to the plants. It looks like shiny bits of foam and can make up to 25 percent of the mix.

Perlite is actually expanded rock but it looks like little bits of polystyrene. It can be added to soil mix and does the same sort of thing as vermiculite.

Compost. Potting mixes usually contain some plant nutrients, but things like small trees will do better and live longer if you stir in some screened compost.

Crocks are traditionally bits of terracotta flower pots that you've accidentally smashed. Place them over the drainage holes in the bottom of containers to prevent blockage. Pebbles do the same thing.

Crushed stone. You can use this for drainage or as a mulch on the compost surface. It shows off ornamental grasses and alpine plants but also deters slugs, which don't like crawling over it.

Polymer granules. Sold under a number of different names, these tiny granules absorb moisture, swelling up to many times their original size. They store water and make it available to the plant during drought, or when you've forgotten to water.

Bone meal. Works well as a slow-release fertilizer and helps to get the plants established.

Tubs, sinks and buckets

You can use absolutely any container if it has drainage holes, holds soil mix and isn't ugly. Garbage cans, ceramic sinks, barrels and galvanized buckets are fine – just drill ½- to ¾-inch holes in the bottom. Porous pots such as terracotta can be painted or varnished inside to cut down water loss, but make sure they're guaranteed frost resistant. Put crocks in the bottom to protect the holes and maybe a layer of gravel for drainage. Use a tree and shrub soil mix and add in bone meal for a slow-release fertilizer; add vermiculite or polymer granules to retain moisture. Standing pots on bricks or those little terracotta feet keeps the drainage holes clear and stops sowbugs and other insects from setting up house underneath.

Half fill with soil mix and press down with your fists. Take the plants out of the pots and place on the compost, filling in around them as you go. Work from the middle outwards. Water in the plants and top up the soil mix if it settles.

Hanging and wall baskets

The perfect thing for small spaces and cheering up ugly walls. Decide where you're going to put them – be sure you can reach them for watering – and then choose a design or theme so the plants and container complement their surroundings. The containers come in a range of shapes and sizes. The plastic ones with built-in drip trays are the easiest to plant and keep watered but the most common are plastic-coated wire baskets.

It's a good idea to carry the same basic design through to all your baskets and maybe even your window boxes and other containers. There are so many suitable plants that you can achieve whatever you want, but as I said earlier, go for interesting plants instead of the run-of-the-mill "Busy Lizzie" nonsense. You may want to stick to a very simple theme with just one type of plant, or a single color, although most people start with some sort of rainbow arrangement and learn from their mistakes.

The earlier in the season you plant the better. For summer planting, go to your garden center and see what's available at the end of the frosts in the spring. It's worth planting your purchases as soon as possible so they get a chance to grow to their maximum potential. Some plants will be labeled as trailing and others as upright; it depends what effect you want but it's a good idea to alternate them within the basket. Top summer plants are osteospermum, *Helichrysum petiolatum*, *Felicia*, *Bidens*, lobelia and geranium.

When the summer is over, it's getting cold and the plants are looking sad, replace them with something for the winter. The choice of plants is relatively limited but try to avoid the pansy route; variegated ivy, ornamental cabbages, heather and other small shrubs are good and most can be used in the garden afterwards. Things don't grow much in winter so you do have to cram them in to get a decent result.

Helichrysum petiolatum

Planting the basket. Choose a spot out of the sun – some sort of bench or table is ideal. Take the basket and undo the chain from two of the three attachment points, using pliers if necessary. Stand it on a flower pot to raise it up. Line the bottom with sphagnum moss or a specially bought liner to hold in the soil mix and moisture. Put a bit of mix in the bottom and stir in some bone meal as a slow-release fertilizer. Remove your bedding plants from their containers and poke the root balls through the liner from the outside. Work around the basket and then put in more moss to line it, followed by more compost and plants, and so on until you get to the top.

Don't skimp on plants but don't overdo it either. There should still be room for them to grow, so if all the root balls are touching it's probably too crowded. Firm the soil mix in well with your fingers as you go and don't forget that it will be seen from below. Put the chain back on, water it in well and check that there is about an inch between the soil mix and the top of the container. Hang it up in a sheltered, sunny spot. See opposite for how to water. You'll never remember from one year to the next what you planted, so write it down or take photographs.

Window boxes

The obvious place to put them is on the windowsill, but try fixing them securely against and on top of walls or railings with suitable brackets. Any container will do but some cheap and plastic ones look nasty and deteriorate in sunlight. The plants are up to you. The extra shelter and warmth from the building might let you grow cyclamen and other slightly tender plants, unless you're on the fifteenth floor of a skyscraper. If it's your only garden space then you may want to grow herbs or even tomatoes and lettuce. Whatever you do, make sure it looks good in summer and then replant for winter. Empty containers are deeply depressing.

Drainage is important. Whatever your container, make sure it has decent drainage holes in the bottom and protect them with crocks. Next put in the soil mix, again mixing in about a quarter of Vermiculite and/or a sprinkling of polymer granules and some bone meal as a slow-release fertilizer. The plants are next. You may want some permanent residents like small-leaved variegated ivy and then more seasonal plants around them for summer and winter. You can also add bulbs for the spring when you're planting it up for the winter. Firm the compost down well by hand and then water it in and top it up if necessary.

Balconies and flat roof tops

It's always a good idea to check first just how sturdy your roof is. A few larger pots are better than lots of small ones – they dry out more slowly. Position them around the edge, above or close to load-bearing walls to prevent nasty accidents. Containers will have to be light so that they don't fall through the roof and so you can move them around. For drainage put a 4-inch layer of gravel or pebbles in the bottom. Don't use soil or loam-based mixes, as they are heavy. Mix in 25 percent vermiculite or perlite to cut the weight further. Try to cut down wind and create privacy with a trellis or some other screening and choose plants that will withstand windy conditions and won't dry out. Good shrubs are escallonia, laurustinus and barberry.

Watering

Watering is *essential*. In warm weather, you may need to do it every day but you can cut down to weekly in cooler periods, especially if you've used polymer granules or vermiculite. Mulching will also cut down water loss, as will positioning things out of the wind and all-day sunshine. To get water straight to the roots, permanently sink a small plastic plant pot with holes in the bottom into the soil mix and fill that with water each time, allowing it to percolate through the mix. If you have a drain-pipe coming off a small roof like a conservatory or shed then feed it straight into a planted container. You'll still have to carry water in drought periods but it cuts down the work. For hanging baskets and other stuff that's high up you can buy a special lance attachment for your hose, or one of those pump-action sprayer things with a curved end part so that the water goes into the container and not all over your feet. When you've forgotten to water your pots and baskets – it will happen – the soil mix dries and shrinks and it's hard to rehydrate. Stand it in a bowl of water, or for less terminal cases add a couple of drops of dishwashing liquid to the water until the mix starts to soak it up normally again.

Vacations are always a problem. Get someone to water while you're away or buy an irrigation system from a garden center. Each pot can have a separate drip feed and the whole lot runs from a computerized timer.

Maintenance

Maintenance of contained plants is relatively intensive – there's no getting away from it: You're growing things in a totally unnatural environment.

— About six weeks after planting, particularly with annuals, start adding a liquid seaweed fertilizer. For flowering plants, a high potash fertilizer is essential and the bag will tell you how much to use.

— Deadhead regularly to channel energy into producing more flowers and remove damaged or dead bits immediately to stop diseases spreading. Treat any pests and diseases promptly.

— Any slightly tender plants like palm trees benefit from some protection in winter. Move them into a greenhouse or conservatory, or wrap the pots in straw, burlap or bubble wrap. Really tender plants can have it wrapped around the leaves but it does look a bit silly.

— Shrubs should be potted into larger containers as they grow but it's not normally feasible. Instead remove as much soil mix as you can from the top and replace it with fresh to give it a boost.

lawns

If you have a shady, postage-stamp garden, or a patch of mud with a few wispy shoots of grass, there's no point fighting it; get rid of it and replace it with a combination of paving, gravel and plants – or just deck it. If the lawn gets some sunshine though, think again.

To many, a garden is not a garden without a lawn. It may only be the size of your bed but that might be all you need to stretch out in the sun or feel the grass between your toes. A lawn can create space but it doesn't have to be grass . . . .

Unusual lawns

Camomile

A camomile (*Chamaemelum nobile* syn. *Anthemis nobilis*) lawn was popular in Elizabethan times. It may not be ideal on a large scale – so if you have lots of space, use it to link together two larger areas of grass or lay stepping stones through a patch. It won't enjoy excessive trampling but when lightly bruised or crushed underfoot the leaves emit an almost appley aroma. All you need is a patch of sunny, well-drained ground. 'Treneague' is a low, tufted variety and is the best cultivar for lawns.

In the late spring fork over and weed the area thoroughly, and then leave fallow for a few weeks. Allow dormant weed seeds to germinate and then remove them as well. Light sandy soils are best, so after a final weed, fork some sand. You can use bought plants or remove the rooted offshoots from established ones. Put them about 6 inches apart and they will spread quickly to form a dense carpet.

They don't totally suppress weeds but you can remove these a couple of times a year. Trim with scissors or shears to keep plants compact and the lawn tidy. Almost every year remove the offshoots and replant to keep the lawn dense, adding a bit more sand at the same time if necessary. Camomile can look a bit sparse in winter so position it carefully.

Thyme

Thyme is seldom grown as a lawn but it's far more robust than camomile. The low-growing *Thymus serpyllum* varieties are best but other taller and bushier types like *T.* x *citriodorus* can form an outstanding scented carpet, although you'll need stepping stones to actually walk through it.

Prepare the ground by forking over, weeding and leaving barren for a week or two.

Fork in horticultural sand, particularly in heavy soils, because the drainage needs to be good. Thyme likes lime so scatter some of that around and scratch it into the surface layer. Use bought plants or divide established ones in spring. Rake the soil level, spread your plants about 10 inches apart and put them in. Water well and that's it. The plants soon knit together. *T.* x *citriodorus* will need cutting back hard with shears or pruners after flowering in order to keep bushy.

Wildflowers

An area of unmown grass at the edge of your lawn can contain wildflowers such as daisies, dandelions,

cornflowers, cow parsley, yarrow, speedwell and white clover to provide nectar and ground cover for bees, beetles, wasps, parasitic wasps and hoverflies. Apart from cornflowers, poppies and a few others, most wildflowers grow best in poor, uncultivated ground, but you can't just leave your lawn to grow long – you have to introduce the right things. Grow them from wildflower seed mixes by raising them in a tray and planting them out individually when small. You can buy the equivalent "plugs" from specialist nurseries by mail order. Choose grassland species that suit your soil: Either test it or have a look at what grows locally. Bird's-foot trefoil, primrose, meadow cranesbill, ox-eye daisy, small scabious, toadflax, wild thyme, marjoram and even spotted orchids may be appropriate. Pull out any unwelcome flowers by hand.

What you plant dictates when you mow. For example, cuckoo flower and cow parsley need to disperse seed for the following year, so don't mow until May. Others like wild marjoram and herb Robert will mean a late summer mow. Cut everything down to about 4 inches, leave for a few days and then rake up and compost the cuttings.

Ordinary lawns

A low-maintenance lawn is achieved in the preparation and planning – you want a lawn for living with, not for looking after, a hard-wearing utility lawn that is a mixture of fine and broad-leaved grasses. Feeding and regular mowing are the keys to lawn success: They make the grass stronger and help to fight off disease and weeds.

Make sure you don't have to carry your mower up and down steps – use a ramp. If you have to carry the mower through the house, or drag it around the side, then you must question the need for a lawn.

First of all, introduce a simple irregular shape (not necessarily a rectangle) that is easy to mow – no tight curves or pointed angles. All of it should get at least some sunshine. Narrow pieces between beds and trees are a problem to get the mower through and little island beds in the middle of the lawn can make the garden look fussy.

Watch out for narrow access points onto a lawn from a path or gate, which can cause excessive compaction and wearing to one area.

Don't put things on the lawn that you have to move every time you mow. Create paved seating areas and put bird feeders and baths in among the planting.

Allow room to maneuver the mower; don't run lawns right up to fences and walls. Don't grass a steep bank – maintenance is a hassle so change the gradient or get it planted with something else.

There's no need to leave a grass-free gully around a lawn. Run grass up to, but slightly higher than, paving or brick edging – and simply run the mower over it. Tidy up with an old knife once a year and the job's done. Plants can be allowed to spill over the lawn edge but if they make mowing difficult prune them back.

Grass doesn't grow well under trees so remove the lower branches or plant bulbs and shade-loving shrubs. If you must have lawn there, use a shade grass seed.

Daffodils, crocus and other bulbs can be naturalized in the lawn, but confine them to specific areas so you can remember where they are. The down side is that you can't cut the grass until the leaves have gone yellow and it can start to look a little messy. Ideally, combine them with wildflower areas around the lawn edge.

New lawns

You will need: spade, fork, landscape rake, rototiller, hose, sprinkler, outside faucet, lawn mower, light roller, scaffold boards, gloves, old bread knife, half-moon edger.

You can lay sod at any time except when the ground's frozen or during a drought, but the best times are autumn and spring – it can then get established right away. It really is hard work, though, so be careful when you're lifting: Keep your back straight and bend your knees.

Getting rid of the old lawn
Mow the grass short and dispose of the clippings. Then with a sharp spade scrape off the grass, weeds and roots, trying not to take too much soil. Turn it upside-down, throw it under trees and bushes as a mulch, or compost it. Leave the soil bare for a few weeks and hoe weeds as they appear. Tap-rooted weeds like dandelions should be dug out by hand. Very small areas can be forked over, but ideally rent a rototiller. Avoid damaging any

tree or plant roots, and go up and down, back and forth until the ground is well broken up.

Laying the sod
Now rake the ground level. Level the soil by eye, working from the back corner to the front. Remove stones and roots. If you're having problems raking, then you may need to rototill again. When it's level, roll it flat, first up and down, then across. Scatter some fertilizer; fish meal or fish, blood and bone meal, a handful every square yard should do it. Give it a light watering and you're ready to go.

Use a good-quality utility sod that will be hard wearing. First, lay a strip of turf around the entire perimeter. Do curves by cutting out little "V"s with an old bread knife or a half-moon edger and bending the sod around. Next, lay the rest of the sod in runs in an interlocking brickwork pattern to fill in the middle; joints should never be next to one another. Work down the garden from the house and always stand on the scaffold boards, flipping them over as you go, which can help to level the area. The lawn will settle down naturally over the next few weeks, but avoid walking on it for as long as possible. When the sod is laid, set up a sprinkler immediately. Moving it without walking on the grass can pose problems but you'll think of something. Don't water during the hot part of the day or the sun will scorch it, and continue watering daily for several weeks or until it looks thoroughly established. Never let it dry out. Dry sod will shrink irreversibly.

Newly laid and regularly watered sod grows really fast for the first few months at least. Make sure

Cornflower

Snowdrop

Daffodil

Crocus

you cut it as soon as it's 1½ inches tall or it'll go all yellow underneath. Don't go on vacation and leave it to dry out or get too long.

Seed

Same preparation but the soil needs to be worked into a very fine tilth. Every stone must go and leveling has to be impeccable. Frost and dew damage seedlings and halt germination so either spring or autumn is best. Subsequent top-seeding is often needed and you must mow it as soon as it reaches 1½ to 2 inches. Using seed is a bit cheaper but only a good solution for patching in or very small areas.

Old lawns

If your lawn is less than 50 percent grass, then it's time to start again. But you can't just throw seed onto an unprepared lawn – it won't grow. To rejuvenate your lawn, cut the grass to about 4 inches and then lower the blade gradually with each cut to about 1¼ inches. Buy bags of lawn top dressing, spread it over the surface, fill any hollows and rake the seed in. Follow the maintenance program rigidly and you'll see a marked improvement.

Simple maintenance guide

A rotary mower is the best because it needs less maintenance than a reel mower and is suitable for any type of lawn. One with a roller will give you stripes. Whatever your mower, avoid stones and manhole covers and sharpen it once a year.

When you water an established lawn, give it a good, deep soaking. Frequent light sprinkles encourage shallow root growth that dries out quickly and burns in a hot summer. In dry weather, let the grass grow longer than usual: If you "scalp" it, it will die.

Mow around the edge of the lawn first, then up and down. Next time go across, or diagonally – cutting the same way every time causes undulations in the ground.

Spring. Do the first cut once the grass is noticeably growing. Keep the blades high – remove just the top down to about 1½ inches. Cut again about three weeks later depending on the weather. Try not to do it when the ground is wet. Start mowing more regularly and in May apply lawn fertilizer to feed the grass and kill weeds. Instructions are on the bag, but apply only when the soil is damp and the grass is dry. Remove any particularly troublesome weeds with a fork, not forgetting the roots, and reseed or sod bare areas. Neaten the edges with a half-moon edger.

Summer. Mow regularly – weekly is best. Trim the edges with shears as necessary. Go – just once – around the edges of paving with a sharp knife. Feed with granular fertilizer and never cut below 1¼ inches.

Autumn. Around September, mow less often and leave it to grow a bit longer. Don't leave fallen leaves smothering the lawn for too long as they'll rot and kill the grass.

Winter. Cut the grass only if it gets long and shaggy, and try to keep off it when it's very wet and frosted.

maintenance

The thing about gardening is that there always seems to be something to do, but in actual fact, as long as you plan properly and choose the right plants, you can get away with doing hardly anything at all – a session each season, near enough. See *The bare-minimum maintenance guide* on page 188.

Weeding

Try to get to know your weeds. All gardens seem to host a small gang of the usual suspects but the complete list of weeds is endless. Annual weeds don't really pose a threat because you can get on top of them easily by hoeing. The ones to watch out for are the tenacious ones that grow and spread from their roots and need to be carefully dug out and dumped – never compost them. The big six:

— Bermuda grass has wiry stems that root wherever they touch the ground. Dig (don't pull) it out and stop it going to seed.

— Bindweed has arrowhead-shaped leaves and aggressive stems that twine around and strangle everything within reach. Even the tiniest bit of root will start a new plant. All you can do is keep after it and wear it out.

— Crabgrass is similar to Bermuda grass and has the same revolting habits. It loves lawns.

— Dandelion has a long tap root and if any piece is left it seems to rapidly regrow with twice the strength.

— Nutsedge is like a grass with triangular stems.

It spreads by seed and stolons (underground roots) and every piece of root you miss will sprout. Dig it out or you'll have it forever.

— Quack grass or couch grass is just an invasive grass that grows where you don't want it and is hell to get rid of. For this and the others, one of those flamethrower gadgets can help – they don't get the roots, but they help you wear out the plant's energy reserves.

Hoeing is the easiest form of weeding but it's strictly a maintenance thing to do when things are more or less under control. There are several different types of hoe and clever people keep redesigning hoes to be more effective. Whichever one you choose, make sure it's robust. You push and pull it through the surface layer of the soil and it basically cuts the weeds down. This is perfect for all the weed seedlings that seem to germinate in the blink of an eye during warm wet weather, but the pernicious fellows like dandelion and nutsedge will keep sprouting up from their roots. Keep a hoe handy by the back door so that you can push it around whenever the mood takes you; by the time you've rummaged around for it in the shed you'll have lost the urge.

Companion planting. There is a bit of myth involved here but there's also a slice of hard fact: some plants stop others from growing. Plant a crop of turnips to wipe out couch grass: It's then far easier to dig out a few unwanted turnips. Lupines keep down just about everything. Give it a try. You can also use companion planting to keep pests at bay (see *Pestilence and Disease*).

Mulching and the no-dig system

It seems that I've been using the no-dig system for years without even knowing it. Basically, you prepare your soil with composts and stuff, plant it all up and then spread an organic mulch over the surface. Repeat the mulch every year and that's it – job done. No mess, no fuss, just mulch. The earthworms and bacteria get on with it and as long as you keep off the soil and don't compact it, then everyone's happy. You can try this even if you have the most appalling soil that is full of weeds. Results aren't instant but if you use a very thick mulch, at least 4 inches, you may never have to do any digging. Think of that.

A mulch can be anything, as I've mentioned already in *Compost*. It is actually best to weed a bed thoroughly first but a decent layer of mulch will keep weeds down and reduce the need for watering, especially with new plantings.

Pruning

Novice gardeners are often a bit cautious with the pruning shears at first, but after a few snips they get well into their stride and turn into psychopathic pruners. Before you let yourself loose, you need to understand why you're pruning and a few of the basic principles. Once you've grasped these, then off you go. There's no need to go into detail about every plant, although there are a few with their own special needs – so we'll cover those individually.

The basics.

— First of all, keep on top of the pruning. If you do a crazed hack every three or four years you'll never get good results and your lanky, misshapen plants will produce mountains of rubbish.

— Pruning off one bit channels the plant's energy to another; you'll get more flowers, more fruit, and although it keeps plants at their required size, it perversely makes them grow more strongly.

— If you choose "no-prune plants" whose size fits their location, then it is possible to have a garden that you very rarely prune.

Tools. You'll need a pruning saw, long-handled pruners, small pruners, shears, gloves and a recent tetanus shot.

Shrubs. As a general rule, if a shrub flowers after midsummer, it should be pruned in early spring. If it flowers earlier in the year, pruning should be done right after flowering.

Shrubs to be pruned in spring: *Buddleja davidii, Caryopteris*, Chinese plumbago, smoke bush, hardy fuchsia, hibiscus, hydrangea, mallow.

Shrubs to be pruned in summer: deutzia, mock orange, lilac, weigela.

What should you prune? Anything that is getting leggy and has open growth will be made more neat and compact by pruning. If something isn't flowering well, then a prune followed by a feed will

Rosa rugosa

Dandelion

often do the trick. Always look closely at the shoot tips. If you're pruning off what looks like a flower bud, think again. If in doubt, prune immediately after flowering has finished – you'll do no harm.

First, dead wood must be cut out and then crossing stems that rub on each other. As low down as possible, cut out up to a quarter of the thickest old stems so they're not all crowded together. Take off any straggly growth and stand back to look at what you're trying to achieve. Always make your cut next to a bud, or pair of buds, but don't cut so close that you risk damaging it. Use sharp tools so that you don't crush the stem and let in diseases.

Don't prune things into neat balls, because they look stupid – you may as well go out and buy some plastic gnomes as well. Keep the shape tidy but try to make it look natural as well.

Be careful. Some plants including California lilac, *Cistus*, broom, veronica and heather can't be cut back too hard. If you cut back into the old wood, they don't like it and start to die back completely. Light trimming is the order of the day.

Some variegated (normally green and white leaves) plants revert back to being plain old green. These shoots have to be removed or the green will spread through the whole plant. It's best to actually tear off the unwanted shoots so that you remove a tiny "heel" from the main stem.

Some plants can be roughly cut with shears to remove the dead flower heads and some of the stem to keep the bush compact. Lavender and aubrieta are good examples.

Dogwoods and willows that have bright red, yellow or green stems in winter should be pruned in late

February or early March. The idea is to cut all the stems back to a low framework about 6 inches high and then a fresh batch of sticks sprout from it. If you don't prune, all the old stems get a bit dull. Every other year is fine.

Trees

The main reason you'll want to prune a tree is to make it smaller and let in more light. Get a professional to look at it if it's verging on the big side, because chain saws are dangerous. If you want to give it a try, follow this simple guide. Decide from the ground which branches to remove or shorten. With a pruning saw take off any damaged wood and any branches that cross. Don't be afraid to take out whole branches, and never just shorten them. You can "raise the crown" by removing all the lower branches, but make sure you still have

a decent shape. Most deciduous trees are best pruned after the leaves have dropped. Legally you can chop off anything that overhangs from your neighbor's garden but think twice; apart from petty neighbor disputes, you might actually benefit from its presence.

Climbers

Most climbers just need a little training: cutting back against walls and winding stems around wires. However there are a few that need special attention.

Clematis. These fall into three categories: The most common are in Group 1, rampant *Clematis montana* types with smallish flowers – the evergreen *C. armandii* and others that flower from January to May. You can leave them alone but all the growth ends up at the top or somewhere in next door's garden. Prune out the shoots every year after flowering or give it a serious hack back to the main framework whenever you get around to it. Many honeysuckles require the same treatment.

Group 2 has large dramatic flowers from late May to early July and often they flower again later. They flower on new side shoots produced from last year's wood. Just trim off weak growth in March to a pair of healthy buds. Good plants include 'Nelly Moser' and 'The President.'

Group 3 flower from July onwards. In early spring cut all the stems back to a pair of strong buds about a foot off the ground and then train the new growth up some sort of support. Favorites include 'Ville de Lyon,' *C. rehderiana* and *C. tangutica*.

A fourth, but unofficial, group which I've just invented is the don't-have-to-do-anything group. They include *C. alpina* and *C. macropetala*. Technically they belong in Group 1 but you can get away with leaving them alone.

Wisteria

Wisteria is a terrific plant but has to be looked after, so you have to decide whether you can be bothered. Wherever you put it, it must have a sturdy trellis or some strong wires to support it. You have to prune twice a year. In January do all the training of the main stems, and then in July you have to cut all the new, rampant green growth back to within 6 inches of the main gray stems.

Herbaceous perennials

Any tall plants that are likely to flop over, such as delphiniums, chrysanthemums and lilies, can be tied to stakes for support. An easier and more attractive solution is to buy a special plastic-coated wire framework. You position it over your plants when they start shooting in spring and they grow up through it and support themselves. Easy.

In autumn or winter, once they look completely dead, cut all the old flower heads and leaves down to about 6 inches. Any shoots at the bottom can be left to protect the plant in winter – and so that you know it's there.

Hedges

Deciduous hedges such as beech should be pruned twice a year to keep them really dense, but you can get away with doing it once in the autumn if you want. For big hedges buy or rent a gas-powered trimmer. Evergreen hedges such as box and yew can be trimmed in late summer or autumn. Small or dwarf hedges can be done easily with hand shears, but laurel hedges should be cut with a pruner – otherwise you chop all the leaves in half and they look dreadful.

Roses

All right, I'll come clean: I hate hybrid tea roses. It's because I've had to look after so many. Savage thorny sticks that attack you when you're just trying to help. Ugly bare stems in winter with bare soil beneath, pest- and disease-ridden plants that lose their flowers in the first puff of wind or drop of rain, constant deadheading, lots of pruning, stuffing thorny stems into plastic bags . . . aaaargh! I hope I've convinced you;

they're a maintenance nightmare. If you insist on having them, don't listen to all that bull about pruning to outside buds and stuff. You'll find that you get perfect results if you hack the whole thing off to just above ground level in early spring. Try old-fashioned shrub roses instead or some of the marvelous disease-resistant climbers and ramblers. Some of them are even thornless.

Deadheading. This is a good general practice for roses, shrubs and perennials that you can do as the mood takes you. Nip off dead flowers between thumb and forefinger or trim with pruners to channel energy into producing new flower shoots. *Rudbeckia* 'Herbstsonne' will flower for at least one more month and roses just keep going.

Pinching out. It's the same sort of thing as deadheading but you remove the shoot tips, which allows side shoots to do their stuff and keep the plants bushy. You can do it to all sorts of shrubs and perennials early on in the year before flowers start appearing.

Protect plants in winter

Any plants that are too tender to endure cold should be protected in winter. Tree ferns, cabbage and other palms may be OK in milder areas or in cities but they don't like the wind and wet, let alone frosts. You can protect trunks with burlap, bubble wrap or straw, and you can even tie all the leaves up together. Other stuff in containers could benefit from the same sort of treatment around their pots to keep their feet warm. Shake heavy snow off branches to keep them from snapping.

Slightly tender plants like gunnera can have the dead leaves cut off and laid over the crown to protect them in winter.

Watering and water conservation

If you must water, the best time to do it is in the cool part of the day, preferably the morning so that the leaves dry off during the day. Wet leaves breed fungus diseases.

Watering daily washes away nutrients and encourages shallow roots, which will dry out at the surface; and it's much better to do it once a week, so the roots grow deep in their quest for moisture. The most economical method is to use a trigger nozzle on the end of the hose, but be careful not to wash the soil away from roots. A sprinkler is gentler and mimics natural rainfall.

To avoid watering, fork lots of organic matter into the soil, and use mulches and water-absorbing polymer granules (see *Compost* and *Containers*).

New trees and shrubs need watering only until they get established and then you can rely on mulches to retain moisture. Lawns do best if you use a mulching mower and water deeply.

As a general rule plants with gray leaves like *Helichrysum*, senecio and *Cistus* have evolved to use less water. Others that like things a bit dry are abelia, California lilac, smoke bush, hibiscus, tickseed, herbs and alpines.

In some situations you'll have to water regardless: container plantings; plants with their roots against walls, in sandy and chalky soils, or on steep slopes; and plants hard up against buildings.

Don't overwater fruit and vegetables because only those with edible leaves need frequent watering. Tomatoes and root crops need a steady supply only when their roots or fruits are swelling. Herbs actually like to be quite dry and even lose some of their scent and flavor if they're too wet.

Simple irrigation systems are easy to set up. You can get a porous hose that sort of sweats water, or drip feeds that accurately supply individual plants and pots. The whole thing can be controlled by a fairly cheap computer attached to your faucet.

Restoring a garden

You can renovate a garden at any time of year but it's probably best in autumn or spring. The soil will be workable but won't be so wet that you'll damage the structure by walking all over it.

If beds are ludicrously weedy then dig salvageable plants out, if they're not too big, and just plant them loosely in a temporary spot. Dig the weeds out and then replant.

Transplant shrubs if they're not too big when they're dormant in spring or autumn (see *Getting Planted*).

Flowering perennials can be dug out and divided (see *Grow Your Own*) and then replanted. In neglected gardens you often end up with one dominating plant: Be ruthless and throw most of it away.

When it comes to pruning don't bother too much about the time of year. Concentrate on shape, size and creating an open framework, and you can bring most shrubs back from the brink. Worry about pruning for flowers next year.

Take cuttings from tired old lavender, root it straight into the ground in September, and junk the parent. Pile soil up in the middle of sprawling thyme and heathers to regenerate growth from the middle.

The bare-minimum maintenance guide

Maintenance, apart from the lawn if you have one, can be cut down to four or five sessions a year if you want. Always work round the garden in a circuit. And while you're at it, check for nasties (see *Pestilence and Disease*).

Spring. This is the most important session – you're waking up the garden for summer. First of all go around and prune all the spring-flowering things and pinch out the tips of other plants. Be careful not to lose your pruners among the garbage.

Next pull out all the weeds by hand and by hoeing. It's a good idea to throw them into a black garbage bag or can and drag it around behind you. Spread compost or fertilizer over the beds and fork it in. Give the lawn a cut and put some fertilizer down a few days later.

On another day do some real gardening. Divide large herbaceous perennials and replant. Sow seed for annuals and vegetables In late spring get your containers planted.

Early summer. Keep cutting the lawn. Do another total weeding of the beds. Prune the spring flowered things as the flowers fade. Deadhead shrubs.

Plant more seeds, bedding plants and vegetables.

Late summer. Feed the lawn. Trim back unwanted growth of hedges and shrubs. Deadhead lilac, roses, *Rudbeckia* and other flowering stuff. Tie and stake perennial plants if they need it.

Autumn. This is when you put the garden to bed for the winter. Remove annuals and bedding plants. Cut down herbaceous plants. Prune hedges. Clear leaves from the lawn and beds. Put garden furniture away for the winter. Feed the lawn.

Plant containers up for winter. Transplant and replant things. Prepare new areas for planting. Plant spring-flowering bulbs.

Early winter. Do a final leaf clearance, adding the leaves to your compost heap. Winter-prune trees and shrubs. Service the mower and store it away. Protect plants and move containers indoors. Have a general tidy-up under plants, etc.

pestilence and disease

If you practice the good gardening techniques in these pages then everything should be fine; the best policy is prevention rather than cure. Use soil conditioners and fertilizers (see *Compost*) to promote strong plant growth and plant things where they are happiest so they won't struggle. A healthy plant wards off pests and diseases.

You will inevitably get minor problems from time to time but follow these basic rules – and keep your fingers crossed.

Pests

Physical control
Get to know which bugs are your friends and which are your enemies. Once you know that, you can destroy the foes on sight: Hose aphids off plants and crush weevils between your fingers, throw slugs into your neighbor's garden and stand on snails. If you can't bring yourself to squash things then keep an old coffee can filled with kerosene, plop them in and they're history. Not very kind perhaps but then this is a book about plants. For the squeamish there are other ways.

Natural-born predators
Most of this is covered in *Birds, Bees and Salamanders,* but what you need to do is encourage anything that will munch pests.

Birds, ladybugs, lacewings, hoverflies, some beetles and different wasplike creatures will between them eat aphids, caterpillars, grubs, scale insects, whiteflies and leafhoppers. Take my word for it – that's

pretty good. Encourage these predators by planting a diverse range of early- and late-flowering plants and ground covers. Don't be too tidy: Leave a little bit of debris and stones beneath plants for bugs to hide in. Some abandoned fruit keeps the wasps happy.

As a general rule don't plant large blocks of one type of plant: Use single rather than double-flowered varieties, wildflowers, different daisies and plants with flowers in umbels – like the spines of an umbrella. Top plants for attracting insect predators are fruit trees, sea holly, yarrow, marigold, fleabane, dead nettle, honesty and mallow.

Don't have areas of bare soil, or beneficial insects will get sunburned and die. Use ground-cover plantings such as geranium and dead nettle for shelter and nectar.

Biological control
If all the above hasn't worked, then you may need to resort to more underhanded tactics. Chemicals aren't in your arsenal so you have to use a natural method. Biological control is the answer.

What you do is call and order a package of tiny creatures. They wing their way to you in the mail clearly marked "live insects," and they have great names like Nemasys H. They'll come with instructions, which often involve mixing them in a can with water and then sprinkling the solution onto your plants. Another method is to hang a piece of prepared card in a bush. It couldn't be easier.

The supplier (see *Buyer's Guide*) will recommend the right bug for you, since each one acts differently. Some, in *Alien* fashion, lay eggs inside the pest; when they hatch, the host is history. Others simply eat the pest. The intention is to set up a balance: Ideally the predators keep the pests on the verge of extinction because if they wipe them out, then they starve. Some predators will need reintroducing from time to time.

Companion planting

This is a great notion for organic gardeners. The idea is that one plant can be planted to benefit another by attracting pest predators, discouraging disease or confusing pests, literally throwing them off the scent and keeping nasties away from your prized plants. Companion planting has its roots in folklore and not all gardeners totally believe it, but it's simple and most of it seems to work.

The outstanding performer is undoubtedly the humble French marigold – a bit bright and some would say rather vulgar but it does have a few tricks up its sleeve. It attracts hoverflies aplenty, which control aphids and deter whiteflies; its smell also confuses cabbage white butterflies, so plant it among tomatoes and cabbages. You can also put it with potatoes where a secretion from the roots will kill spud-munching eelworms. And yes, there's more: Pop marigolds into a bed of couch grass and they'll even de-weed that for you. There are more weed-combating planting companions and you'll find them in *Maintenance*.

Plant carrots and onions together to disguise their individual smells. Carrot and onion flies get confused and go elsewhere. Chives, catmint, parsley and thyme will keep aphids off roses. Basil keeps whiteflies off tomatoes and sweet peppers and allegedly improves their flavor.

Permitted pesticides

These are considered organic chemicals because they're derived from natural sources. Most importantly, if used carefully they do no harm to the bugs that we want to have around. They're available from garden centers and the most useful ones are insecticidal soap and Neem, which zap the common insect pests and are active for only a day, but be careful because they may harm friendly ladybug and hoverfly larvae. Derris and pyrethrum are even less discriminating and if you use them for caterpillars and insects then some of your allies could fall victim to friendly fire. Caterpillar problems can best be solved by using the appropriate kind of *BT* (bacillus thuringiensis), which kills caterpillars and nothing else.

Disposing of stuff

Dump or burn any part of a plant that you even suspect of being infected by something nasty – never be tempted to throw it on the compost heap. Give your pruners a wipe on your trousers or disinfect them so you don't pass the disease on to something else.

Hall of shame

Slugs and snails
Simply the worst pests. Slime trails, devastated hostas (plantain lily) and munched leaves. Encourage birds, salamanders, frogs and toads. Sink stale cups of beer into the ground as traps. Salt's always good and a packet of slug nematodes is the absolute best.

Aphids
Greenfly and blackfly, in other words. You're bound to see these pests whatever you do. They suck sap from tender parts of plants, especially new shoots and leaves. Rub them between your fingers, hose them off, use insecticidal soap and encourage birds and other predators. Aphids excrete honeydew which is sticky stuff that attracts ants. It then grows a black fungus called sooty mold.

Caterpillars
If you want to attract butterflies then you must suffer their caterpillars. Remove them by hand or destroy infested plants. Some species hide behind silky threads and curl up the leaves around themselves. The biological control is a bacterium spray of *Bacillus thuringiensis*.

Whiteflies
A tell-tale cloud of tiny white bugs fly up when you brush a leaf. You often find them on house plants and in the vegetable garden, but they're not a problem to most ornamentals. Greased sheets of yellow card can be hung in bushes to trap them.

Vine weevils
These evil weevils are on the increase. Faintly striped browny gray beetles chomp the leaves while underneath their maggoty grubs devour the roots, causing the plants to wilt and topple. Destroy on sight. Dip entire pots into derris solution. Dump infected plants and soil, and disinfect pots. Send off for some nematodes, or spray BTSD.

Earwigs
Ugly brown things with pincers for a tail, they do eat a few enemies like codling moth larvae, but they also eat the flower buds of clematis and other plants. Make traps by stuffing straw into a flower pot and upending it on a cane among the plants. They hide inside, but don't forget to empty it and then kill the beasties.

Spider mites
Really a houseplant or greenhouse problem but dry weather might lure them into the garden. They live on the flip side of leaves and they're very small and orange, pale green or yellow. Fine webbing and silvery mottling on the leaves give them away. Treat with insecticidal soap, or introduce the predator *Phytoseiulus persimilis*.

Carrot, onion and other flies
It's generally the larvae that do the damage. They burrow into roots, particularly root vegetables, anything cabbagey, radishes and parsley. Plants wilt, foliage discolors and seedlings die.

Get your revenge by hoeing regularly to expose them to the birds and use companion planting to confuse them.

Cucumber beetles

There are two kinds of these devastating pests: spotted and striped. The spotted kind is also known as the southern corn rootworm; its larvae feed on corn roots, killing or weakening plants, while the adults attack leaves and blossoms of squash family plants, other vegetables and flowers. The striped cucumber beetle zaps squash, beans, corn, peas and garden flowers, bores holes in fruit, and carries wilt and mosaic viruses. Its larvae feed on the roots of squash family plants, usually killing them. You can control both kinds of beetles by covering young plants with floating row cover – remove it when the plants flower – or by buying parasitic nematodes.

Cutworms

Green or gray-brown caterpillars that live in the top layer of soil. They come out at night and feed on root vegetables and the leaves and stems of herbaceous plants, cutting them off at ground level – hence their name. Hoeing the ground exposes them to predators and a biological control is available.

Wireworms

These are the larvae of click beetles. They are quite common and eat holes in vegetables, particularly root crops. If you're only an ornamental gardener they might do a bit of damage to the odd bulb or perennial but won't cause much concern. Burying lumps of potato or carrot as traps can help. Mark where they are by putting a stick into them. Dig them up every couple of days and throw them in the garbage.

Ants

Ants are actually quite useful in the garden because they help to ventilate soil and eat a few pests as well. Everyone hates them though so if you want to deter them get greasebands from the garden centre to put on the stems and trunks of plants, and spray nests with a mixture of pepper and garlic. Spearmint, lavender, sage and hyssop can be put by doors to stop them coming into the house.

Sowbugs

These little armadillo-like fellows that can roll themselves into a ball are kind of interesting to look at but they are not good for plants. They live in dark, damp places and come out at night and eat roots, stems and leaves, causing big, uneven holes. Being tidy and clearing debris is the solution but you might be getting rid of friendly bugs as well. Some sort of compromise is in order.

Millipedes

These are usually black and have many legs. They live in the soil surface and occasionally eat plant roots and bulbs. Don't confuse them with the fewer limbed, friendly brown centipedes. Disturbing the soil by forking or hoeing exposes them to predators, but on balance they do more good than harm.

Flea beetles

Hot dry summers make this tiny jumping thing very happy. It'll attack seedlings, vegetables and nasturtiums, leaving plants looking shot-gunned with hundreds of small, randomly spaced holes on the young leaves. Good garden hygiene helps, especially in winter, and they can be trapped with sticky yellow cards placed among the plants.

Codling moth

Mainly a pest of apples, but also pears and other fruit trees, the caterpillars of this moth are the most common cause of maggoty fruit, with holes surrounded by brown powdery droppings. In midsummer, wrap the trunk in a sticky band to trap larvae, or release parasitic wasps.

Diseases

The same goes for diseases as for pests: vigilance and cleanliness are the key. Don't pack plants too closely or diseases will spread, and remove sick-looking leaves as you notice them. Keep a good healthy garden with strong plants and you'll suffer few problems. Avoid particularly susceptible plants that attract a host of diseases, such as roses, and you'll scarcely have to worry.

Companion planting is also useful to minimize diseases. Sweet peppers prevent foot and root rots so try planting them among your ornamentals. If you really get into growing vegetables then a bit of crop rotation wards off evils.

Botrytis or grey mold

Probably the commonest disease, this is a fuzzy fungus like the one that grows on bread. It spreads easily, affects lots of plants and can be very troublesome. Infection occurs through wounds and dead bits of plants. Brown spotting or blotching is followed by the mold. Good hygiene, removing dead flowers and leaves, and all that stuff helps. Remove any infected parts ASAP.

Rust

Rust looks exactly like it sounds. Orange, brown or black spots appear on the leaves and stems, making the plants quite ugly and, in some cases, causing death. Remove and dump any infected leaves, especially at the end of the season, to prevent overwintering. Persistently infected perennials should be dug up and thrown away. Potassium deficiency encourages it – apply potash.

Leaf spot

A fungus that not surprisingly causes spots on leaves, especially roses. It can usually be prevented by proper fertilizing and clearing debris. Remove infected leaves, prune hard in autumn and spray with copper fungicide.

Mildews

Spots and patches of a white powdery or downy layer of fungus appear on leaves and stems, often causing the plant to wither and look a bit rough. Prune the plant to allow better air circulation, keep it well watered and mulched, and avoid wetting leaves. Spray with copper fungicide. Some plants just won't shake it off; get rid of them and plant something resistant.

Mosaic virus
A yellow mottling of leaves, particularly of tomatoes, leaf vegetables, cucumbers and squashes. Growth may be stunted. As for all viruses there is no cure. Prevent spreading by destroying infected plants and controlling the aphids that spread it. Tobacco mosaic comes from smokers' hands, so keep smokers out of your garden.

Foot and root rots
Bedding plants, especially geraniums, seedlings, tomatoes and cucumbers can be susceptible to this fungus. It causes discoloration or blackening at the base of the stem, which shrinks in and rots. Plants wither and die. Use sterile soil mix for seedlings and cuttings, don't overcrowd and water with copper fungicide. And plant sweet peppers.

Damping off
Damping off is a similar fungal disease to rots, affecting seedlings. Avoid overwatering and crowding.

Wilts
These diseases become depressingly visible when stems and leaves droop and turn yellow, then brown. The lower part of the plant is usually affected first. Infected plants often die. There are two fungal wilts with similar symptoms: verticillium wilt, and fusarium wilt. There is no cure for either one, and infected plants should be removed immediately, before the infection spreads, and destroyed by burning or dumping. Plants affected include tomatoes, peppers, melons, several flowering species, fruit trees, and woody and herbaceous perennials. There are wilt-resistant cultivars of some plants. Crop rotation does not seem to help, but soil solarization (covering soil in hot weather with clear plastic so that the soil is "cooked") is sometimes effective.

Bacterial wilt shows itself when plants droop and go limp. Infected plants are soft at first, but then turn hard and dry. If you cut a stem, you may see long, sticky strands of white bacterial ooze. Cucumber beetles and grasshoppers spread bacterial wilt, so protection is possible with floating row cover material, or by planting resistant cultivars. Destroy infected plants as quickly as possible.

Fireblight
This is a serious bacterial disease that affects apples, pears and ornamental shrubs including pyracantha and cotoneaster. It enters the plant through flowers, and leaves turn brown, giving a scorched appearance, particularly at the ends of branches. Remove infected bits, cutting back 6–12 inches of healthy material, and burn immediately. Sterilize pruners between cuts with a 10 percent bleach and water solution.

buyer's guide

The way most people buy plants is to wander around a garden center on a Sunday and make impulse buys. Often they get home, leave their new plants on the deck for a while – to dry out and topple over – and then try to figure out where the hell they're going to plant them. What you should do is plan ahead, and if you don't know exactly what you want to buy, you should at least have a particular location in mind.

The plants in this book are all fairly easy to come by and a garden center is the best source.

People in the U.S. spend millions of dollars every year on garden plants and landscaping. With that amount of money flying around, it's important to spend your cash wisely. There's a lot of good stuff out there but there's also a lot of garbage, so *caveat emptor* and all that.

Buying plants

Garden centers. I always have a good look around a garden center. If it's smothered in weeds and generally messy then I leave it alone. Plant hygiene is everything: If the plants are old and unwell they'll take years to settle in and recover.

The plants are grown at nurseries, and as soon as a plant arrives at a garden center it starts to deteriorate. In many cases it may be very slow, negligible in fact, but in the nursery the plants have been grown in optimum conditions and the garden centers can't emulate them. The way around this is to go to a place with a very high turnover, where plants haven't been sitting around

for a long time, and to follow this simple guide.

— The plant should look strong, with a good shape and no straggly or snapped branches. The leaves should be sprightly rather than dull and limp.

— Even if you think the plant looks healthy, have a quick look under the leaves for any sign of pest and disease. You may not know exactly what you're looking for but if you have any doubts, don't buy it.

— The pot should be free of weeds. This is a good indicator of how long it's been standing around and the general level of housekeeping. If you buy a weedy plant you'll be introducing the weeds to your garden as well.

— Shove your finger into the pot. If the soil is dry rather than moist then put it back down and walk away.

— Turn the pot upside down. Are there roots sticking out the bottom? Turn your back to the staff and ease the pot off: there should be roots and soil visible. If all you see is roots then it's pot bound and unhappy. If all the compost falls on the floor then it's a young plant that's just been "potted on." You've also just made an embarrassing mess and it could be time to leave.

Size isn't important. If you have the cash, it is sometimes worth buying large, contained plants. If you want to instantly screen something, or you want a specimen plant for a large pot, then this could be the way forward. A few large shrubs in a newly planted garden give it an instant air of maturity and it may be the only option if you want a plant that grows at a snail's pace.

On the other hand the prices are sometimes quite terrifying – hundreds, and even thousands of dollars for one plant. Large plants always take longer to settle in and establish so you can often lose a year or two anyway. Some plants just aren't worth buying big because they grow quite quickly anyway. A good example is eucalyptus. You can buy a 6- to 10-foot tree and lavish love and attention on it, or you can buy a twig barely 2 feet tall, and within two or three years they'll both be the same height.

Some places sell extremely tiny shrubs. They may be quite handy for window boxes – but, really, they're a waste of time.

Nurseries, catalogs and shows. Retail nurseries actually grow the plants that they sell, and they can be cheaper, especially if you buy in largish quantities, when you may be able to haggle a bit on the price. There aren't too many of these near towns and cities but if you pass any on your travels it's often worth stopping in for a look. They aren't as flashy and organized as the big garden centers but they know their stuff and they often sell interesting plants.

If you're after anything unusual, something you spotted on vacation or saw on TV, then it can be a headache to get hold of it. Specialist nurseries are the answer, and many will send you their catalog free.

Seeds and bulbs are available from garden centers but all the seed companies produce catalogs, and they're easy to order over the phone. Mail order is big business for growing plants as well. The prices are often quite cheap and there are certainly some bargains to be had, but size and quality can be sacrificed. I think there's something not quite right about getting plants through the mail and I've heard lots of unhappy tales, but some people swear by it. It's up to you.

Garden and flower shows are always a good place to buy plants. Take a look at the calendar of events in any gardening magazine to find a show nearby.

The list of companies on page 202 is by no means comprehensive but will give you an idea of what is available.

Seed companies

W. Atlee Burpee & Co.
Warminister, PA 18974
800-333-5808
FAX 800-487-5530

General seed catalog and an heirloom
seed catalog.

The Cook's Garden
PO Box 535
Londonderry, VT 05148
800-457-9703
FAX 800-457-9705

Seeds and supplies for the kitchen
garden.

Johnny's Selected Seeds
1 Foss Hill Road
RR 1 Box 2580
Albion, ME 04910-9731
207-437-4395
FAX 800-437-4290

Wide selection of organic vegetable and
flower seeds.

Peaceful Valley Farm Supply
PO Box 2209
Grass Valley, CA 95945
888-784-1722
FAX 530-272-4794

Organic vegetable, flower and green
manure seeds.

Shepherd's Garden Seeds
30 Irene Street
Torrington, CT 06790-6658
860-482-3638
FAX 860-482-0532

Vegetable and flower seeds; garden
supplies.

Seeds of Change
PO Box 15700
Santa Fe, NM 87506-5700
888-762-7333
FAX 888-329-4762

Organic seeds for heirloom varieties.

Plant nurseries

Miller Nurseries
5060 West Lake Road
Canandaigua, NY 14424
800-836-9630
FAX 716-396-2154

Fruit and nut trees, berries, some
flowers.

Henry Field's Seed & Nursery Co.
415 North Burnett
Shenandoah, IA 51602
605-665-4491
FAX 605-665-2601

Vegetable and flower seeds and plants;
fruit, nut and shade trees.

Tools and supplies

Gardens Alive!
5100 Schenley Place
Lawrenceburg, IN 47025
812-537-8650
FAX 812-537-5108

Organic insect traps, insecticides,
fungicides, fertilizers; lawn seed; floating
row covers.

Gardener's Supply Company
128 Intervale Road
Burlington, VT 05401
800-863-1700
FAX 800-551-6712

Fertilizers, irrigation equipment, tools,
general supplies.

Lee Valley Tools Ltd.
PO Box 1780
Ogdensburg, NY 13669-6780
800-871-8158
FAX 800-513-7885

Seed-starting supplies, quality tools,
equipment and supplies.

A.M. Leonard, Inc.
214 Fox Drive, PO Box 816
Piqua, OH 45356
800-543-8955
FAX 800-433-0633

Tools for professional and really serious
gardeners.

Seeds of Change
PO Box 15700
Santa Fe, NM 87506-5700
888-762-7333
FAX 888-329-4762

Catalog of top-quality imported tools,
plus bird and bat houses, seed-starting
equipment and books.

Peaceful Valley Farm Supply
PO Box 2209
Grass Valley, CA 95945
888-784-1722
FAX 530-272-4794

Organic soil supplements, fertilizers and
insecticides; beneficial insects, books
and general supplies.

Smith & Hawken
2 Arbor Lane, Box 6900
Florence, KY 41022-6900
800-776-3336
FAX 606-727-1166

Top-quality imported tools and
equipment; request *Tools of the Trade*
catalog.

Magazines and books

Horticulture
98 North Washington Street
Boston, MA 02114
800-234-2415

Published eight times a year; 1-year subscription $26.

Kitchen Garden
63 South Main Street, PO Box 5506
Newtown, CT 06470-5506
203-426-8171

Published bimonthly; 1-year subscription $24.

National Gardening
180 Flynn Avenue
Burlington, VT 05401
800-727-9097

Published bimonthly; 1-year subscription $18.

Organic Gardening
33 East Minor Street
Emmaus, PA 18098
800-666-2206

Published eight times a year; 1-year subscription $19.96.

The Organic Gardener's Handbook of Natural Insect and Disease Control; Barbara W. Ellis and Fern Marshall Bradley (eds.); Rodale Press, 1992. ISBN 0-87596-124-X.

Heirloom Vegetable Gardening; William Woys Weaver; Henry Holt & Co., 1997. ISBN 0-8050-4025-0.

The New Organic Grower; Eliot Coleman; Chelsea Green, 1989. ISBN 0-930031-22-9.

(There are, of course, thousands of books on plants and gardening. Libraries, Internet booksellers and your local bookstore will help you find what you want.)

Help and advice

Your local County Cooperative Extension agent is a good source for climate information (first and last frost dates, for example) and growing information on all sorts of plants. Agents used to promote chemical solutions to everything, but in recent years most have seen the light and now offer organic advice, too.

State universities that have agricultural and horticultural programs are often willing to point you in the right direction for help with specific problems such as insects and diseases.

Local libraries can help you find gardening clubs which, in the hope that you will become a member (there are worse things to join), may give you some free advice. Their meetings are a good way to meet other local gardeners.

Before you hire anyone for serious landscaping work, check them out with the local Better Business Bureau and members of a local garden club, and ask them for some references to people they've done work for. Your favorite nursery or garden center might have some thoughts on the subject, too. Big machines, trees and work crews are mighty expensive, so be cautious.

index
Main entries are in bold.

USDA Plant Hardiness Zone Map

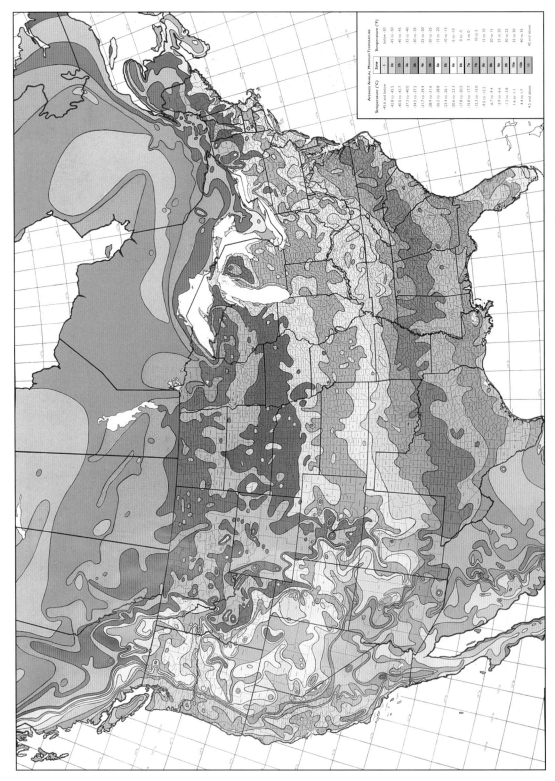

Map courtesy Agricultural Research Service, USDA